Seasonal Activi[ties]

Spring & Summer

Caroline Matusiak

Bright Ideas
FOR Early Years

Published by Scholastic Publications Ltd,
Villiers House, Clarendon Avenue,
Leamington Spa, Warwickshire,
CV32 5PR

Written by Caroline Matusiak
Edited by Catherine Baker
Designed by Sue Limb

Illustrations by Gloria

Photographs by Caroline Matusiak
(pages 5, 9, 10, 27, 41, 56, 71, 83) and
Bob Bray (page 55)
Cover photograph by Martyn Chillmaid
Cover designed by Sue Limb

Artwork by David Harban Design,
Warwick

Printed in Great Britain by
Loxley Brothers Ltd, Sheffield

The publishers wish to thank Pitman
Publishing for permission to quote 'I had
a little cherry stone'.

A catalogue record for this book is
available from the British Library.

ISBN 0-590-53000-3

Contents

For Rosalind Helen

Introduction

Spring and summer bring new sights, sounds and sensations for exploration.

The changing weather of early spring presents daily surprises, with late frost, winds and rain giving way to the sun that announces the season of growth. The appearance of green shoots in the ground and buds on the trees gives rise to observation and discussion, and stimulates interest in the planting and nurturing of seeds.

As summer approaches and the plants mature, the children watch and comment on the insects that visit the flowers. Summer is also a time for visiting the seashore which, with its sand, shells and creatures, offers another environment to experience and enjoy.

The seasons pass with a predictable regularity, and yet they never lose their freshness and appeal.

Seasonal topics

The ideas offered in this book are intended as starting points to be adapted according to the needs of the children. When planning topic work, it is useful to have a selection of activities to work from, but be sure to provide scope for the children to determine the direction of the topic. The children will readily suggest areas of particular interest, and these can be successfully followed.

Topic work requires careful planning. Having planned the curriculum, you need to observe to what extent the children's needs are being met and what they are actually doing, saying and experiencing. These observations lay the foundations for staff interaction with the children, and provide the information required for record-keeping. The final stage of topic work is the evaluation of the provision, activities and experiences children have been offered during the topic. These evaluations influence future planning. The cycle of planning, observing, interacting, record-keeping and evaluation continues to ensure that activities are appropriate and meet the needs of the children.

Planning the curriculum

There are several factors involved in the successful planning of topic work.

Activities

These will require planning over different time spans.

- A year plan covers the number and nature of topics, to avoid duplication and to make the best use of seasonal variations and the festivals associated with the different seasons.
- A term plan provides the overall plan of a specific topic, taking into account the curriculum areas covered.
- A weekly plan takes into consideration the sharing of equipment and space in a school community. For example, computer work, baking and movement may need to be allocated to certain days depending on the availability of equipment. Additional activities to extend children's experience can be planned for all areas, for example, finger painting and bubble prints in the paint area.
- A daily plan ensures that the appropriate resources and staff are available to undertake the activities.

All planning needs to be responsive to the children's own interpretation of the equipment and activities, and to the direction of their thinking and learning.

Equipment

The provision of equipment needs to be planned for all areas and activities. The equipment must present the opportunity to practise and refine different skills as well as offering scope for social, physical, emotional and intellectual development.

Time

Plan for the efficient use of time. Transitions from one activity to another take time with large groups of young children, and should therefore be kept to a minimum. A routine that is predictable and yet flexible helps children and staff to participate with independence and confidence.

Space

Space needs to be used efficiently and effectively. Certain areas, such as those for paint, water and sand, require a non-slip surface and proximity to a water supply. The book corner and writing centre need to be sited in a quiet area with carpeting and good light.

Roles and responsibilities

Staff and parents need to know their role and area of responsibility. Some activities are adult-intensive, for example, baking, and these will require an adult to be present all the time. At other times, staff can oversee a larger number of activities, supporting and extending children's own ideas.

Observing

Observing children involves watching and listening as they play. It is important to have a defined focus for the observation. Here are some suggestions for observation:

- Observe an individual child, to find out how he relates to peers and adults, to identify the areas and activities he chooses as well as those rarely or never chosen, and to note the willingness and skill with which he communicates with others.
- Observe a group of children, focusing on social skills. Are they co-operating or is each child following her own course of play?
- Observe an activity, to see how children actually use the materials provided. Are they the source of imaginative, social or physical play?
- Concentrate on one area, for example, the writing centre, recording how many children visit it, which equipment they use and how. Are some materials constantly moved to another area? This reflects the need for the re-siting of equipment.

There are different methods of observing children's play. One method is to use 'random time samples', observing for ten minutes every hour. Longer periods of sustained observation are difficult to maintain, but can be worthwhile when you require detailed information about a child in order to assist him.

When observing, it is vital to take brief notes; otherwise, essential information will be forgotten. All staff need to observe and compare notes on a child to give an all-round picture of her development.

Interacting

Decisions regarding equipment and activities are based on the information gained during observation. The nature of staff intervention in children's play depends on the areas of need observed and noted. One child may require encouragement to use language, another may lack the confidence to participate, while a third needs a challenge. Staff should share observations, so that their approach is consistent and yet open to the changing needs of the child.

Record-keeping

Staff observation and interaction with children provide the basis for record-keeping. Records are a means of monitoring a child's progress, describing social, intellectual, physical and emotional development. It is important that all staff contribute to the record-keeping so that no important information or significant development is overlooked.

Invite parents to share in the observation of their child, and welcome their contributions.

Evaluating

Resources, including time and space, need constant evaluation. Aspects of nursery activity such as water, sand and outdoor play will require examination to ensure that resources are stimulating and well-maintained. Activities and experiences that are successful, as well as those that prove less fruitful, need to be considered with a view to extending children's experiences. This evaluation needs to be systematic and continuous.

Getting started

It is important for staff to work as a team, sharing their observations and ideas relating to all areas of the curriculum. Start by planning activities and experiences that give children opportunities to use their five senses and develop an understanding of the world around them. The seasons offer a wealth of valuable activities which will stimulate children's curiosity and act as a springboard for their thinking and talking. The sights and sounds of the season are waiting to be explored and enjoyed.

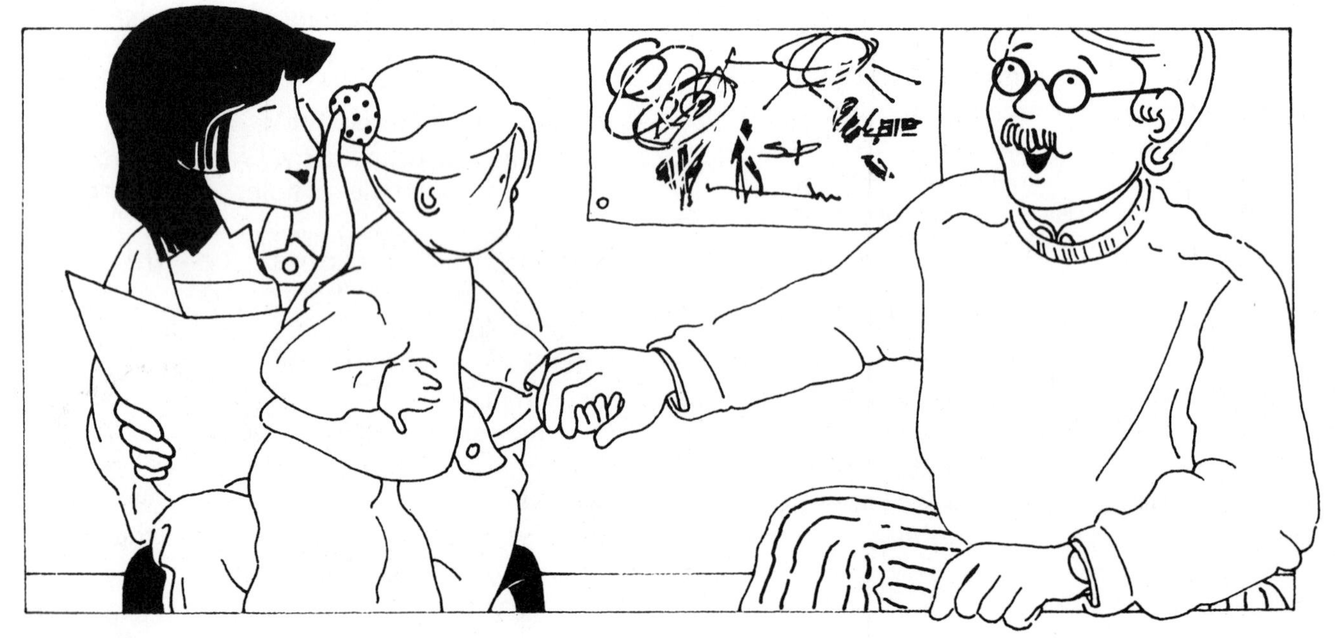

Spring

Spring is the time of growth and new life, when seeds germinate and young animals are born. During spring, children have an opportunity to consider families, both human and animal, and to learn to share responsibility for the care and nurture of living things.

The well-being of new living things is determined by the weather, which is constantly changing at this time of year. The dependence of seeds on rain and sun can be explored in the garden and in the classroom, and through exploring the weather children will discover more about the properties of water and air.

The topics for this season are 'Growth', 'Homes and families' and 'Weather'.

Growth

Chapter one

Young children are fascinated by the appearance of new life, from germinating seeds to hatching chicks. A visit to the nursery grounds or local park draws attention to the sights and sounds of spring. If possible, allocate a space outdoors where the children can plant seeds and observe their growth.

Inside, the children can plant seeds in a variety of containers, and vary the conditions as they investigate the need for water and light. The life-cycle of the seed can be photographed and recorded, and children can observe and taste some of the seeds we eat.

Let's visit the nursery grounds

Objectives

Science: understanding how living things are looked after, and observing seasonal changes.

What you need

Access to the nursery grounds or a local park, small-sized garden tools, a selection of quick-growing seeds.

What to do

Walk around the park or nursery grounds looking for signs of spring, including new growth on twigs and green shoots in the soil. Recall how the leaves fell from the trees and how the bulbs were planted during the autumn. Look at the fallen leaves still remaining. How have they changed over the winter? Perhaps there are some leaf skeletons that can be taken into the nursery for close examination with a magnifying glass. Encourage the children to look at the pattern and symmetry of the veins.

Introduce the gardener who works in the nursery grounds or park, and watch as he or she digs, rakes, plants, mows the grass and trims the hedges. Discuss the work in the garden or park at different times of the year.

Wearing plastic gloves, the children can help to clear old leaves and litter in the school garden, as long as this does not entail handling sharp or dangerous objects.

If you have a suitable patch of ground available at the nursery, set it aside for class use. Otherwise plant seeds in large pots outside. Let the children choose some seeds for planting from a mixture of flowers and vegetables that are hardy and quickly grown, for example, marigold, nasturtium, radish and spring onion. Encourage the children to prepare the ground and sow the seeds themselves under supervision, using small-sized garden tools such as rakes, shovels and wheelbarrows. Any large stones and irregular patches of seedlings will provide points for future discussion.

The children may sow seeds in rows if there is space, but if not it is easier to sow them in clusters. Dig any compost or leaf mould made during the autumn into the soil, and put some over the young shoots to protect them from frost.

The children can observe the progress of the seeds over a period of time as they water and tend them. Dig up some flowers and vegetables at different stages for the children to observe both root and shoot growth. Leave others to seed.

Talk about

Signs of spring, buds, leaves, shoots, flower and tree names, gardening tools, planting seeds.

Follow-up

Science

- Set up a wildflower area in part of the nursery grounds. Packets of wildflower seeds are available, and many of these flowers attract insects such as bees and butterflies. This is useful for the topic on minibeasts (see Chapter 4).
- Discuss the litter which is dropped in the grounds, usually sweet and crisp packets. Who drops this litter? When? Is the litter bin sited in a useful place on a main thoroughfare?

Maths

Let the children grow sunflower seeds and chart their growth on a strip of card. Compare the height of a sunflower with that of other objects: smaller than a flowerpot, taller than the fence, the same height as Mary.

Let's discover seeds and plants

Objectives

Science: knowing that living things reproduce their own kind, and recognising the parts of a plant.

What you need

A sharp knife for adult use only, white paper, magnifying viewers, a selection of flowers such as hyacinth, tulip and daffodil, perhaps from bulbs planted by children in the autumn.

What to do

Let the children observe the colours of the flowers, and the shape of the petals. Ask them to smell the fragrance. If they look inside the daffodil's trumpet, the tulip and the small hyacinth florets, what can they see? Why do they think these are there? Which insects do they think would fit inside the flowers? What happens when they brush the stamens on a piece of white paper?

Cut through a daffodil and a tulip lengthways for children to examine the inside of the flowers. Encourage them to look at and compare the shapes of the leaves; the broad tulip leaves and the long, thin daffodil ones.

Let the flowers go to seed. Day by day, the children can watch as the seed containers swell and the petals wither and fall. Cut through a seed pod from each flower. With the children, look at the tiny seeds. What colour are they? Sprinkle some on white paper inside a magnifying viewer. Seal the lid to ensure that children do not attempt to taste.

Talk about

Flowers: colour, shape, number of flowers, stalk, petal, leaf, seed, bulb, stamen, pollen.

Follow-up

Maths

Ask the children to look for flower patterns on fabrics, for example, on curtains and clothes.

Technology

Using collage materials including tissue paper and crêpe paper, the children can design and make a flower.

Science

Take the children to visit a local florist or nursery to look at varieties of plants and find out about their care.

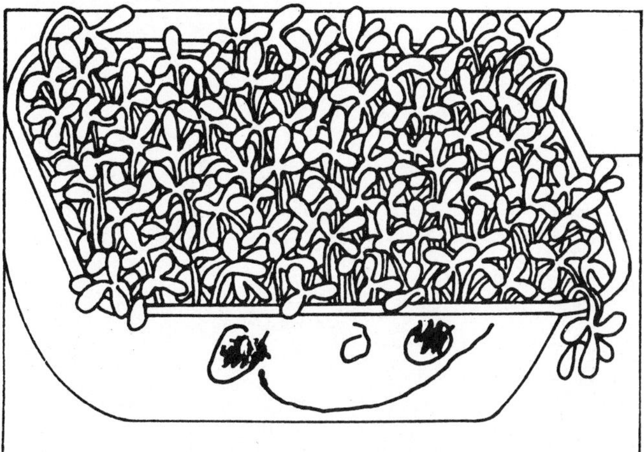

Planting seeds

Objectives

Science: observing that plants need certain conditions to sustain life.
Maths: considering the concept of time.

What you need

Sticky-backed paper, cress, mustard or grass seeds, blotting paper, felt-tipped pens, containers of various types, for example, plastic trays, egg cups, margarine tubs and detergent bottle lids.

What to do

Invite each child to draw a face on the sticky-backed paper with felt-tipped pens. Peel off the backing and stick the face on a container of the child's choice. Place blotting paper at the bottom of each container and sow the seeds on top. Grass seeds take longer to germinate than mustard and cress, and provide a useful comparison.

Cover the seeds with dark paper and let the children water them regularly; see 'Watering the seeds', page 14. Remove the paper when the seeds germinate. The growing seedlings become the 'hair' for the face.

Talk about

Growing seeds, containers, water, germinate, light, dark, a long time, a short time, each day, yesterday, tomorrow.

Follow-up

Science

When sowing the seeds, leave one container without water and compare the results. Ask the children what seeds need. How are seeds in the garden watered? Discuss rain.

Watering the seeds

Objectives
Maths: thinking about time.
English: writing for a purpose.

What you need
Coloured poster paper, scissors, felt-tipped pens.

What to do
Cut out the shape of a twig with leaves from the poster paper. Invite a different child to water the seeds each day. When the seeds have been watered the child can write her name on a leaf. This will help ensure that everybody takes a turn.

Talk about
Each day, daily, first, second, next, the last person, everybody.

Measuring seedlings

Objective
Maths: measuring with non-standard units.

What you need
Seedlings, strips of coloured paper, card, scissors, adhesive.

What to do
As the seeds germinate and grow, let the children measure them at intervals with strips of paper, which can then be cut to the appropriate size. Mount these strips of paper on card in sequence. Draw a simple illustration of the seed on or beside the card strip each time it is measured. Fast-growing seeds such as cress can be measured daily and the measurement linked to a day of the week.

Talk about
Measures: how high? Longer than, shorter than, the same length.

Mung beans

Objective
Science: observing that plants need certain conditions to sustain life.

What you need
Mung bean seeds, an unbreakable transparent container, muslin or fine net, string or an elastic band.

What to do
Place the mung beans in the plastic jar. Cover the open top with muslin or net and secure this in place with string or an elastic band. Let the children rinse the seeds by filling the jar with water and then emptying it; they should do this several times. Ask them to take turns to water the seeds daily.

Mung beans are interesting not only to grow but also to taste. They should be ready in five to seven days, and the resulting beansprouts can be eaten raw or stir-fried on their own or with other vegetables.

Talk about
Bean, root, shoot, water, swell, long, longer.

Follow-up
Science
- Try growing runner bean seeds in a plastic jar. Place the beans between the jar and a piece of rolled blotting paper for easy viewing.
- Plant the seedlings out in a pot or in the garden and let the children watch how high they grow.

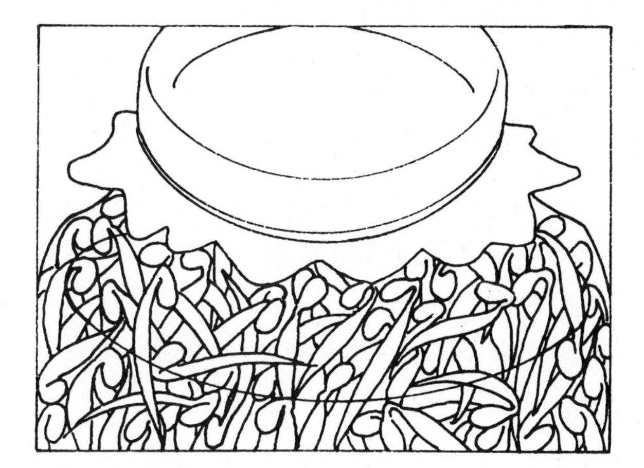

Twigs

Objectives
Science: investigating seasonal change.
Maths: observing change over a period of time.

What you need
Twigs from a variety of trees and bushes.

What to do
Choose twigs with buds of different shapes and colours, for example, the sticky bud of the horse-chestnut, the black bud of the ash, and others. Select some twigs that will blossom, for example, apple and cherry. Twigs from willow, hazel and alder are interesting because they produce catkins.

Place the twigs in water. Encourage the children to observe the buds daily, looking for changes as the buds open.

Talk about
Trees, twigs, buds, leaves, blossom, shape, size, colour, a long time, at first, next, later.

Follow-up
Science
Look for buds opening in trees and bushes.

Observational drawing

Objectives

Science: observing and recording.
Maths: thinking about time, number, shape and size.

What you need

Paper of different colours, drawing materials including crayons, charcoal, pastels and chalk, a budding twig or seedling.

What to do

Place the twig or seedling on the table. Discuss with the children its colour, size, number of buds or leaves and any other attributes. Encourage children to discuss their own observations. For example, Alex noticed a cluster of aphids on the underside of a leaf and said they looked 'like ice'.

Introduce the drawing materials and paper, inviting children to record their observations. Talk with the children as they draw. Their observations are often perceptive and always individual.

Talk about

What does it look like? How many? What shape, colour? What else can you see?

Follow-up

Science and maths

Repeat this activity at a later date and encourage the children to note and record any changes in the twig or seedling.

Dandelion

Objectives

Science: investigating the processes of life.
Maths: thinking about the concept of time.

What you need

A dandelion plant, soil, a plant pot.

What to do

Let the children plant the dandelion in the pot and water it regularly. They can observe the way it changes over a period of time. In due course, plant some of the seeds and let the children watch as they grow. Encourage the children to take other seed heads into the garden, blow the seeds away and watch as they are carried on the wind.

Talk about

Dandelion, leaves, flower, seeds, blown by the wind.

Dandelion clock

Objective

Science and maths: recording changes over a period of time.

What you need

Cardboard, scissors, a paper-fastener, felt-tipped pens.

What to do

Fix a pointer on to the middle of a large square of cardboard, using a paper-fastener so that it will move like a clock hand. Divide the card into quarters. Draw a picture of one stage of the dandelion's life in each quarter: the seed lying on the ground, a plant with leaves, a plant with leaves and a flower, a plant with a seed head. Use the 'dandelion clock' to discuss with the children the way the plant changes as time passes.

Talk about

What happens? What happens next? Now, then, afterwards, before.

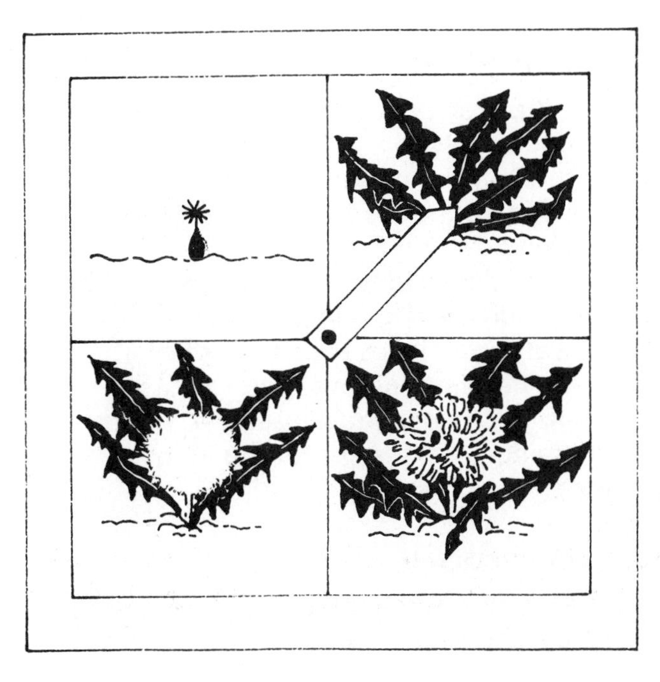

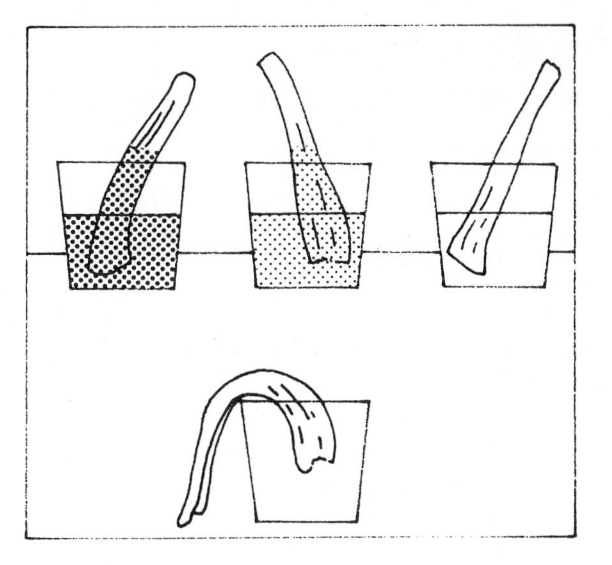

Celery sticks

Objective

Science: investigating the processes of life.

What you need

Celery sticks, four transparent containers, water, red and blue food colourings.

What to do

Let the children stir red food colouring into the water in one container and blue colouring into another. They can add water but no colouring to the third container. They should leave the last container without water, and place a celery stick in each container.

After an hour or two, ask the children to observe the colour change in the celery sticks placed in the coloured water. They can try to trace the passage of the water in the celery sticks. The celery stick in the empty container will quickly become flaccid.

Talk about

Why? What can you see? What does it feel like? Colours, water.

Moss garden

Objective
Science: observing the variety of life.

What you need
Moss, flowers such as daffodil, narcissus and scylla, small twigs in bud, a container such as a bulb bowl, margarine tub or seed tray, pieces of bark, stones, foil, small figures and model animals, a magnifying glass.

What to do
Let the children place the wet moss in the container, and gently cover the stems of the flowers and bases of the twigs with moss. The wet moss provides the plants with water.

Ensure that the children water the moss garden regularly. With the magnifying glass they can look at the feathery and star-like patterns made by the moss, and they will be able to observe the tree and flower buds as they open.

Pieces of bark, stones and small models can be added to make a miniature garden. A piece of foil makes an attractive pond.

Talk about
Patterns, looks bigger, star-like.

Watering can

Objective
Science: investigating the properties of water.

What you need
A water tray, a small watering can, a flowerpot, a sieve, a colander, a slotted spatula, a perforated serving spoon, a skewer, transparent and opaque plastic bottles.

What to do
Use the skewer to make holes in the plastic bottles. Vary the level and pattern of the holes, for example, make a row up the side, round the top or underneath the bottle.

Invite the children to use the water tray and equipment to investigate the passage of water as it takes the shape of its container, finds its level and flows through any available aperture. Which containers hold water for the longest time?

Talk about
Water, names of containers, flow, trickle, spray, shower.

Follow-up

Science

Let the children water the garden with the different containers. They will need to wear waterproof aprons for this. Which container is the most effective?

Jack and the beanstalk

Objective

English: listening and responding to a story.

What you need

A felt board, felt of different colours, scissors, PVA adhesive, a needle, cotton.

What to do

Using the felt, cut out the story characters: a small Jack, a giant and his wife. It is useful to cut out other key features such as the beanstalk, the gold and the harp. The figures need only be quite basic. Leave plenty of scope for children's imagination.

Tell the story using the felt board and figures, and ask the children to predict what will happen next. Discuss the different versions of the story. When children are familiar with the story, encourage them to make up their own alternative endings. Is the giant friendly or fierce? Does Jack climb the beanstalk again? Who does he meet this time?

Leave the felt board and story figures in the book corner. This gives children the opportunity to retell the story and make up their own versions.

Talk about

What happens? What happens next? Story language, for example, 'Once upon a time, a boy called Jack . . .'.

Follow-up

Maths

Use the story to help the children compare for size, for example, the huge giant and small Jack. They could also consider height, for example, climbing up and down the beanstalk.

Beanstalk height chart

Objective

Maths: measuring with non-standard units.

What you need

Ready-mix paint, a tray, a large and a small pair of wellington boots, large sheets of paper or a roll of wallpaper, a 'beanstalk' with leaves cut from green poster paper fixed from floor to ceiling.

What to do

Put the paint in the tray. Secure the paper to the floor or table with masking tape to keep it still and let the children place a boot in the tray and print it on to the paper. Leave the prints to dry and then cut them out. Mount these boot prints up the centre of the beanstalk with the small prints set beside the larger ones.

Invite the children to stand up against the beanstalk to measure their height in boot prints. How tall are they? Count and compare 'Jack' prints with 'giant' prints. The leaves of the beanstalk can also be used as a unit of measure.

Talk about

How tall? Taller than, shorter than, the same size, how many? Number names, the first, second, third leaf.

Seeds from food

Objective

Science: investigating the variety of life.

What you need

A magnifying glass, a sharp knife for adult use, fruit or vegetables with seeds that are eaten, for example, tomatoes, cucumbers and courgettes.

What to do

Take two tomatoes and let the children observe them. Ask the children what colour the tomatoes are. What does the skin feel like? Let the children smell the tomatoes. Where do they think the tomatoes were attached to the plant? Cut one tomato in half vertically and the other horizontally to reveal a different pattern of seeds. Ask the children to look at the seeds and the patterns they make.

Cut each tomato in quarters. Remove some seeds and let the children look at them with a magnifying glass. What colour, shape and size are they? Where do they grow? Encourage the children to taste the tomatoes.

Repeat this on another occasion using a different fruit or vegetable. Save some seeds for comparison.

Talk about

Seeds, their shape, size, colour, location, pattern.

Follow-up

Science

Grow some tomato plants in a bag of appropriate compost. These will flourish in a sunny position. The children can water them regularly, chart their growth and taste the resulting tomatoes.

Salad

Objective

Science: observing the variety of life with all five senses.

What you need

A sharp knife for adult use, a dish, radishes, lettuces, spring onions and other salad vegetables, possibly grown in the nursery garden.

What to do

Ask the children to wash their hands, and then shred the lettuce with their fingers. Cut the radish into rings, and let the children look at the red outer skin and compare this with the white inner flesh. Chop the spring onions. Mix the vegetables together in a dish and let the children taste the salad.

Talk about

Salad: what does it look, smell and taste like? Where does it grow? On top of the soil or underneath the soil?

Follow-up

Science

Try using different types of leaves, for example, Chinese leaf or red cabbage.

Rice salad

Objectives

Science: observing with all five senses the seeds we eat, and observing the effects of heat.

What you need

Rice, fresh, frozen or canned sweetcorn, peas and carrots, see-through saucepan.

What to do

Explain that rice is a seed, and let the children observe the grains of rice, noting their colour and texture. Boil the rice in the transparent saucepan while the children watch, and leave it to cool. Ask the children if they can see any changes in the rice. Boil the sweetcorn, peas and carrots, and leave these to cool. Mix the vegetables and rice together in a dish and let the children taste the salad.

Talk about

Colour, shape, texture, hard, soft, small, larger.

Seed shakers

Objectives

Science: investigating sound and observing seeds.

What you need

Containers such as yoghurt pots, margarine tubs and gravy tins, seeds such as grains of rice, barley or wheat, dried peas or beans, conkers, peanuts and walnuts in shells, paper, masking tape, coloured paper, scissors, PVA adhesive.

What to do

Let the children each choose a container and some seeds, and place the seeds in the container. Ask them to seal the top with a lid or with paper and tape. Children often find it easier to handle masking tape than sticky tape.

Let the children cut and stick coloured pieces of paper on the outside of their containers to decorate them. They can compare the sounds made by the small grains and the larger nuts.

Use these shakers to accompany songs and rhymes.

Talk about

Seeds: grains, barley, rice, lentils, nuts, walnuts, chestnuts, peanuts. Sounds: rustle, shake, soft, loud.

I had a little cherry stone

Objective

English: speaking and listening.

What to do

Encourage the children to say a rhyme they know to a small group of people.

I had a little cherry stone [curl a finger]
And put it in the ground, ['plant' in the other hand]
And when next year I went to look,
A tiny shoot I found. [uncurl finger]
The shoot grew upwards day by day, [raise finger]
And soon became a tree. [spread the fingers]
I picked the rosy cherries then [pick cherries with the other hand from the 'tree']
And ate them for my tea. [raise fingers to mouth]

Hatching eggs

Objectives

Science: observing the processes of life and looking after living things.
Maths: considering the concept of time.

What you need

An incubator, perhaps borrowed from a local school or teachers' centre, fertilised eggs, chick meal, milk.

What to do

Before hatching eggs it is necessary to find a home for the chicks. The children will enjoy seeing photographs of the chickens as they grow to maturity.

Place the fertilised eggs in the incubator. They need turning several times a day unless the incubator is self-turning. The eggs need a constant temperature of 37.5°C and take three weeks to hatch. Monitor the water level to ensure that the humidity is maintained. The progress of the eggs can be seen when they are candled or illuminated on a Cellascope.

Children are thrilled to watch the eggs as they hatch. They soon recognise an egg that is about to hatch when it starts to rock gently. They are surprised to see how wet and large the chick is as it emerges. Tired chicks that sprawl over the floor of the incubator can cause concern until children realise that they are merely resting. The wet, tired and newly-fledged chick soon becomes fluffy, chirpy and energetic.

After hatching, the chicks need to be taken to their new home or placed in a box with sawdust with an overhead infra-red lamp to maintain their body temperature. At this stage their food includes chick meal and milk. Detailed instructions should be available with the incubator.

Talk about

Equipment names and purposes, temperature, humidity, fertilised, hatch, beak, wings and other parts of a chick, wet, fluffy.

Follow-up

Science

- Visit a working farm that welcomes school parties, or invite a vet or farmer to bring a hand-reared lamb to school.
- Set up a butterfly habitat, and let the children watch as the eggs hatch into caterpillars. Ensure that fresh supplies of the caterpillars' food plant are readily available.

Pancakes

Objectives

Science: observing the effects of heat.
Maths: measuring with standard units.

What you need

2 eggs, 225g flour, 1 pint milk, 50g butter or margarine, lemon, castor sugar, bowl, juice squeezer, sieve, spoon, whisk, frying pan, spatula.

What to do

Shrove Tuesday brings the opportunity to cook with eggs. Let the children help as much as possible with the squeezing, measuring and mixing.

Squeeze the lemon and sieve out the pips. Measure the flour into the bowl. Add the eggs and half the milk to the flour, and whisk them all together well. Add the remaining milk, and whisk again. Leave the mixture to stand for a short while.

Melt the butter in the pan. Add a little batter and cook it until it is golden brown underneath. Toss or turn the pancake and let it cook on the other side. Cover the pancake with lemon juice and sugar, and let the children taste it. This mixture makes approximately 12 pancakes.

Talk about

Ingredient names, squeezing lemon, juice, sieve, runs through, melt, batter, crisp.

Follow-up

English

As you work, say this rhyme:

Mix a pancake,
Stir a pancake,
Pop it in the pan.

Fry the pancake,
Toss the pancake,
Catch it if you can!

Let's look for green and yellow

Objectives

Science and maths: matching and sorting by colour.

What you need

A selection of green and yellow objects, including natural and living things such as daffodils, crocuses, chrysanthemums, jasmine, forsythia, lemons, apples, kiwi fruit, melons, pears and seedlings, and man-made items such as toys, plastic household and gardening equipment.

What to do

Talk with the children about the colours of the objects. Can they think of other green and yellow things? Observe the shades of yellow and green.

Talk about

Green, yellow, names and attributes of items.

Follow-up

Science

Let the children try mixing shades of green using blue and yellow powder paint. They should start with yellow, and add a little blue powder and then a little more. They can watch as the colour changes. Let them repeat the experiment using blue as the starting point.

Science and maths

Ask the children to sort different types of materials that are green and yellow, and mount these on a large sheet of paper as a collage. Display the collage as a background to the discovery table.

Homes and families

Chapter two

Spring is a time for new life and growth, bringing the opportunity for children to consider human development. A new baby brother or sister can be invited into the nursery, and older siblings can demonstrate their reading and writing skills. The children can look at photographs of themselves as babies and discuss how they have changed.

The freshness of new buds brings the urge to spring-clean the house. The children will discover the functions of household machines as they clean, wash and cook. At a time when birds are nesting, children can consider different types of housing and build homes using a variety of materials.

Let's meet a family

Objectives

Science: introducing the stages of human development.
Maths: thinking about the concept of time.

What to do

Invite a family to meet the children, either as a group or individually. A new baby brother or sister can be bathed, fed and changed with the older child helping, to avoid jealousy.

Ask grandparents to bring in photographs of themselves as children. Ask them to talk about their childhood days, pointing out the differences in toys, clothes and games played. Ask them to bring in a toy from their childhood. It may be possible to extend this by visiting a local museum or inviting the curator to show some antique toys to the children. Grandparents may have skills that they can demonstrate, or they may prefer to spend time informally in the nursery, talking and playing with the children. It is important that grandparents and fathers become a part of nursery life to help break down stereotyped role models based on age or gender.

NB Many children live in single parent families or with guardians. It is important that all children feel that their family unit is accepted and valued.

Talk about

Stages of human development: baby, toddler, child, teenager, adult. Family members: brother, sister, father, mother, aunt, uncle, grandparent.

Follow-up

Science

- Invite parents to make or bring food that is eaten at home so that children can taste food from different cultures.
- Ask parents to contribute simple recipes to the nursery cookbook.

English

Ensure that the role-play area has cooking equipment and clothing that reflect a multicultural society.

Guess who?

Objectives

Science: investigating the stages in the human life-cycle.
Maths: thinking about the concept of time.

What you need

Photographs of the children when they were babies and as they are now, photographs of staff as babies and teenagers, card and punched plastic sleeves to fit a file.

What to do

Ask parents and carers to bring in two pictures of their children; a baby photograph and a more recent one. Mount the pictures of the children on card with the recent photograph set beside the baby one for comparison. Mount staff pictures in a similar way. Protect the photographs with a plastic sleeve and clip them into a file.

Talk about

The stages of human development: baby, new-born, toddler. Age: six months, one year, two, three, four years.

All about me

Objective

English: using a word processor to produce text with the teacher as scribe.

What you need

Word processor with large font print-out, printer, paper, crayons or felt-tipped pens.

What to do

Invite the children to talk about themselves and their families. As they talk, type what they say on a word processor. Show the children the keys to be pressed for the letters of their names. Discuss the keys and watch the type appear on the screen from left to right. Demonstrate the delete key. Print out the work immediately to ensure that children observe the whole process. Read the print-out together. The children can draw pictures to illustrate their text.

Mount these sheets in a personal book for each child. Other ideas for the book include hand- and footprints, a self-portrait, the child's name and other early mark-making. Read these books with the children and encourage them to write and draw in them.

Talk about

Writing, word processor, screen, printer, keyboard, typing, print-out, disk.

Follow-up

Maths
Draw round the children's hands and feet on card. Use these cards for ordering and matching by size.
Science and maths
Draw round children of different ages and round a member of staff. Compare the outlines for size.

Read me a story

Objective
English: listening to stories.

What you need
Older children, including the brothers and sisters of children in the nursery, story books.

What to do
Invite some older children to read favourite story books to one or two nursery children in the book corner. This gives younger children an opportunity to enjoy books and to be presented with a model of young readers. It gives older children a valuable opportunity to practise their skills in a meaningful way.

Talk about
Favourite stories, reading, pictures.

Animal families

Objective
Science and maths: classifying according to different categories.

What you need
Sets of plastic zoo, farm and domestic animals.

What to do
Invite the children each to choose an animal and then find its young. Together, name the adults and the young. When children are familiar with this, invite them to sort the animals according to other categories, such as zoo and farm animals, birds and animals, those that live in water and those that fly.

Talk about
Animal families, names, attributes.

The three bears

Objective

Maths: comparing and ordering by size.

What you need

Three bears of different sizes (either from jumble sales or borrowed from the children), a box to fit each bear as a bed, an old curtain cut into a simple pillow and cover to fit each bed, three different sized plastic containers for bowls, three boxes to fit the bears for chairs, a doll the same size as baby bear for Goldilocks.

What to do

Tell the story of Goldilocks and the three bears using the doll and teddies. When you refer to the bears, mention their size, for example, 'the tiny baby bear'. Match Goldilocks with the furniture and compare for size, so that one bed or chair is 'too big' and another 'too small'. As you tell the story, introduce expressions of size, for example, 'bigger than', 'smaller than' and 'the same size'.

Invite the children to help find the cover and pillow that fits each bed. At the end of the story match each bear to its bowl, chair and bed. Leave the bears and their furniture in the book corner to encourage children to retell the story and create their own tales.

Talk about

Comparing for size, taller than, ordering by size, tall, taller, tallest, short, fat, thin.

Sound effects

Objective

Science: making sounds in a variety of ways.

What you need

A drum, a chime bar, a triangle, a tambourine.

What to do

Tell the story of Goldilocks and the three bears, using a drum to accompany the large bear, a tambourine for the middle-sized bear, a triangle for the tiny bear and a chime bar for Goldilocks. For example, 'Goldilocks saw that the door was open and crept into the house . . .' (slow beats on the chime bar) and 'Suddenly, Goldilocks woke up and ran out of the house . . .' (quick, light taps on the chime bar). Adapt the sounds made by the instruments to suit the story.

When the children are familiar with this, invite four children to accompany the story with the instruments. Play guessing games, for example, say 'One of the bears looked into the bowl . . .' and play one of the instruments, so that the children have to guess which bear it was.

Talk about

Making sounds, instruments, voice, loud and soft sounds.

Let's visit the locality

Objective

Science and technology: observing the types and uses of materials in familiar situations.

What to do

Take the children on a walk to look at housing in the vicinity of the school. Identify the types of houses: flats, bungalows, terraces, semi-detached and detached. Identify and name the parts of a house: door, window, guttering, roof, window-sill and step. What do the children think is the function of these different parts? What are they made from? Together with the children, identify and name the materials: brick, tile, glass, wood and cement. Look at the patterns of the brickwork and tiles.

Look together at the shapes of houses, windows and doors. Compare various features for size, for example, the garage door is wider than the front door. Can the children say why? Identify and name the colours of parts of the house. Which rooms are upstairs? Which rooms are downstairs?

How can the children tell whether a house is old or new? Perhaps there is ornate plasterwork or something distinctive about the house. Look for signs of birds' nests in roofs and gutterings.

Talk about

Houses, types, materials, parts, rooms, age.

Follow-up

Maths

Ask the children to look for and identify the house numbers.

English

Encourage the children to look for and read the street names and any other environmental print, for example, posters, bus stops or 'For Sale' signs.

Making maps

Objectives

Maths: considering two and three dimensions and location.

What you need

A large sheet of paper, thick felt-tipped pens of different colours.

What to do

Place the paper on the floor. Discuss a prominent feature in the locality that is well-known to the children, possibly a shopping precinct, and draw the road on which it is situated. Ask children to name shops and other buildings in the area, and as they do so, draw these in on the map as an oblique or side view. Encourage the children to draw in other places they know, perhaps a letter-box or car park.

Write in the names of shops and other places. The children will also enjoy drawing pictures of themselves or their cars on the map. Write captions to help orientation.

Talk about

Where? Next to, in front of, behind, on the corner, opposite.

Sand bricks

Objectives
Maths: learning about shape and space.

What you need
Wet sand, brick moulds or margarine tubs, a trowel or spade.

What to do
Encourage children to fill the moulds with wet sand and make sand bricks. When they can achieve this, encourage them to build a wall. Ask them to consider how they can make a strong wall.

Talk about
Shape, fill a mould, fit together, row, on top, side by side, close together.

Follow-up
Technology
Invite a parent who is a bricklayer to demonstrate these skills to the children. Alternatively, watch as builders work in the nursery or neighbourhood, keeping at a safe distance.
Maths
Tape thin paper to a wall and let the children make brick rubbings using the sides of wax crayons. Encourage them to observe how the bricks bond.

Let's discover houses

Objective
Science and technology: designing and making model houses using a variety of materials.

What you need
A variety of construction materials including LEGO, Duplo and Mobilo, scrap materials, a choice of fastenings including sticky tape, PVA adhesive, paper-clips and thread.

What to do
Invite children to design and make a house using construction materials of their choice. Display these houses on a road with small vehicles and figures. Card houses can be stapled to a display board featuring a road or other locality such as a green space or precinct. Cut a large 'V'-shaped flap in the back of three-dimensional box models and staple this to the display board for easy mounting.

Talk about
How? What sort of? Roof, door, window.

Follow-up

Maths

Invite the children to look carefully at their models and draw plans. Listen as they talk about shape and number. Observe how they draw their plans and the features that they incorporate. Write captions to explain these ideas for parents.

Science

Observe a deserted bird's nest. Bake the nest in the oven to kill any insects. Discuss the materials including straw, twigs, moss and threads. Observe how they are neatly woven together.

The three little pigs

Objective

English: retelling known stories using puppets.

What you need

Four wooden spoons or paper bags, fabric, coloured paper, sticky tape, PVA adhesive, thread, three houses (see page 34).

What to do

Make some puppets to represent the three little pigs and the wolf. To make wooden spoon puppets, tie some fabric underneath the bowl of a spoon for clothing. Stick on coloured paper shapes for the face, or paint a face on the back of the spoon. Fasten paper ears on to the spoon with tape. To make paper bag puppets, tie some string over the corners of a paper bag for the ears. Stick on shapes cut from coloured fabric or paper for the face.

Tell the story using the puppets and the houses. Let the children choose names for the puppets; you may also ask them to decide on the pigs' gender.

Folk tales are part of our oral tradition and vary with each telling. Listen to the children's suggestions and discuss the various possibilities. Do the pigs all live happily ever after? My children decided that the third little pig was a girl and that she rescued her brothers.

When the children have decided what happens, retell the story using the new version.

Talk about

What happens next? Story conventions such as 'Once upon a time'.

Follow-up

Maths

Number the pigs and their houses. Use cardinal and ordinal numbers when referring to the pigs: one, two, three; first, second, third.

Where does it belong?

Objective

Maths: sorting objects.

What you need

A bag or box with an assortment of household objects, for example, a toothbrush, a spoon and a pillowcase.

What to do

Describe one of the items in the bag to the children. Ask them to guess what the object is. If necessary, give further clues, perhaps describing the object's function. When the children have named the article, ask them which room in the house it belongs in.

Talk about

Colour, attributes such as texture and shape, features such as handle and bristles, names of articles and rooms.

Follow-up

Maths

Invite the children to cut out furniture and household items from mail order catalogues. Using a thick felt-tipped pen, divide a large sheet of paper or card into rooms. Invite the children to sort their pictures and stick them in the appropriate room. Some items will be specific to one room, for example, a bed, while others, such as a clock, may belong in several rooms. Discuss this with the children as they make their choices.

Sounds

Objective

Science: listening to a variety of sounds.

What you need

A cassette recorder with cassette, household objects.

What to do

Record a range of familiar household sounds, or buy a pre-recorded cassette of these sounds. Play the cassette to the children and ask them to identify the item that makes each sound.

Alternatively, make the sounds using actual household equipment behind a screen. For example, you could jingle some cutlery and ask children to name the objects that make that sound.

Talk about

Sounds, making sounds, names of household objects.

Household machines

Objectives
Science and technology: considering household appliances that use electricity and understanding that misuse of electricity is dangerous.

What you need
The school vacuum cleaner, washing machine, cooker, refrigerator and other appliances.

What to do
Introduce these appliances by focusing on them during a relevant activity. For example, during a baking session, ask the children to look at the cooker before it has been turned on, and when storing food, consider the fridge. At an appropriate time, perhaps when the carpet is covered with sand or small pieces of paper, borrow the vacuum cleaner. Plug it in and clean the carpet.

Ask the children to think about what these machines are used for. How do they work? Discuss sockets, plugs, leads and the dangers associated with electricity and electrical appliances.

Talk about
Household machines, their function, how they work, when we use them, electricity and the dangers it brings.

Follow-up
Science and maths
Invite children to cut out pictures of household machines from catalogues. Which ones are used in the kitchen? Which are used in the garden?
English
In the home corner, provide equipment that resembles household machines.

Spring cleaning

Objective
Science: considering the uses of water.

What you need
Dressing-up and dolls' clothes, washing powder, water and bowl or water tray.

What to do
Invite the children to help with washing the nursery equipment. It is most practical to carry out this activity in the water tray. Wash some of the clothes in warm water, and later add some washing powder. Ask the children how they can get the clothes clean. How do they think they can get them dry?

Talk about
Washing, clean, stains, washing powder, water, drying.

Follow-up

Science and technology

With the children, look at household machines. They can watch while an adult irons the clothes, taking safety precautions. On another occasion, let the children watch while you wash clothes in the washing machine, or take them to a local launderette. Discuss the function of household machines and warn the children about the dangers of electricity.

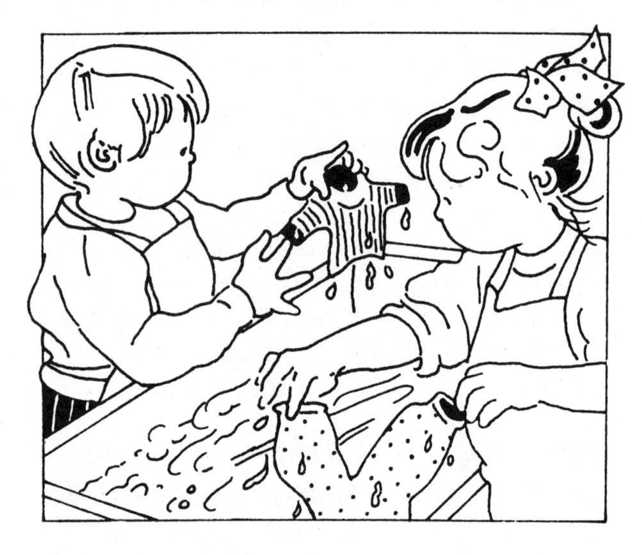

Neighbours

Objective

English: speaking and listening in an imaginative context.

What you need

A divider or screen, home corner equipment.

What to do

Divide the home corner to make two houses. Discuss with the children who lives in each house. Perhaps a baby lives in one. What does he need? Who looks after him? Who lives in the other house? Perhaps an elderly person? Is it the grandmother? What does she need?

Listen to children's suggestions for equipment. Improvise or make simple items from card, such as glasses to help the elderly person to read the paper. Parents with young babies may be able to donate baby equipment. Provide suitable babycare equipment for the nursery doll, and suggest that the children give it a name. This will encourage them to look after it.

Consider the multicultural and gender dimensions of role-play. Is relevant equipment available? Are boys and girls encouraged to take a caring role?

Talk about

Neighbours, next door, families, family members.

Follow-up

English

Place a range of printed material in each house: papers, catalogues, books and samples of junk mail. Include writing materials such as memo pads, pools coupons, envelopes and catalogue forms. This encourages reading and writing behaviour.

Designing on fabric

Objective

Maths and technology: finding out about space and shape.

What you need

Plain light-coloured material such as sheeting, a sewing machine or needles and thread, fabric crayons, an iron.

What to do

Measure the fabric to fit the home corner window, and sew the curtains. Encourage the children to participate in this. Invite them to draw pictures on the material with the fabric crayons. When their pictures are finished, you can iron over the pictures to set the crayon.

Other articles which can be designed and made for the home corner include cushions, tablecloths and tea-towels.

Talk about

Covering an area, the right size, fits, too small, too big.

What's the time?

Objective

Maths: thinking about the concept of time.

What you need

A circle of card, a paper-fastener, card for the clock hands, scissors, felt-tipped pens, adhesive, a mail order catalogue.

What to do

With the children, cut out pictures representing times of the day, for example, breakfast, nursery, lunch, home, tea and bedtime. These pictures may show items or actions associated with a particular time. Discuss the pictures with the children. Divide the card 'clock' into equal sections. Paste an appropriate picture in each section. Secure the hands with a paper-fastener.

Mount the clock at child height in the role-play area. Encourage the children to turn the hands of the clock to the appropriate time of day during imaginative play.

Talk about

What time is it? Time to wake up, go to bed, go to nursery, meal times and daily routine, clock, tell the time.

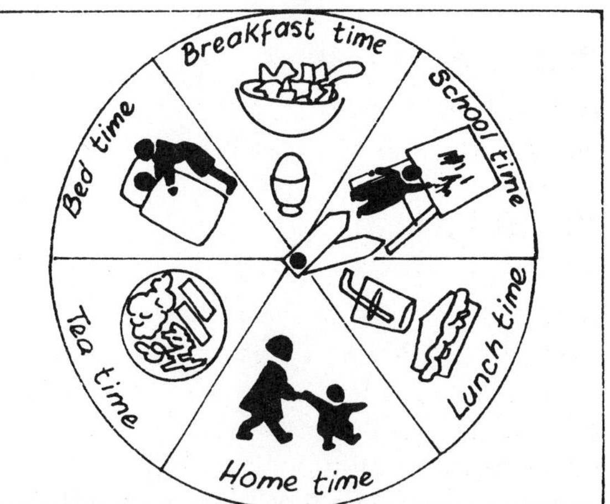

Making dens

Objective

Maths and technology: designing and making a house to accommodate children.

What you need

Lengths of fabric, for example, old curtains and sheets, large crates or construction blocks.

What to do

Encourage children to design and make 'houses' for themselves as a focus for later imaginative play. Fabric lengths are useful for roofs. The crates can be used for walls or furniture, and household equipment from the home corner can be introduced as required.

Talk about

What sort of . . .? How? What shall we use? Where shall we put it? Do you fit inside? Is there enough room for you and your friend? Too small, the right size, room for one more.

Weather

Chapter three

Spring brings the opportunity to experience rain, wind, ice, fog, sun and frost, and changes in the weather can be recorded on a daily and weekly basis. Observing a rainbow in the sky leads to making rainbows in the nursery. As children examine puddles and hang out washing, they can watch the action of the rain and sun, which introduces the topic of water and evaporation.

The changing weather turns children's attention to the clothes and shoes that keep them dry, warm or cool. Children can watch as the seedlings they planted are watered by the rain, and can collect rainwater to measure how much has fallen. Windy days bring the opportunity to test kites and windmills, showing the direction and force of the wind.

Weather-watching

Objective

Science: observing the variety of weather conditions.

What you need

A washing-up bowl, a cup, magnifying glasses, hoops.

What to do

With the children, visit the nursery grounds in different weather conditions. Look at the effects of sun, wind, rain, frost and snow on natural and man-made features. Let the children observe as the rain soaks into the ground in the garden, watering the grass and seedlings. They can watch as it forms puddles on pathways and flows into gutters and drains.

Place a washing-up bowl outside. After a rainfall, bring it into the nursery and pour the rain water into a non-standard measure such as a cup. Ask the children how many cupfuls there are. When it is freezing outside, bring the bowl of ice in for the children to observe. When the sun shines, let the children observe the empty bowl. Ask them why there is no water in the bowl. When it snows, bring the bowl inside for children to feel the snow, observe it with magnifying glasses and watch as it melts.

On a sunny day, encourage the children to look at the shadows cast by familiar objects. They could move a hoop in different ways and watch the shadow change. Encourage the children to twist and turn to make and change their own shadow shapes.

Encourage them to discuss the clothes they are wearing to keep warm, dry or cool. Introduce the idea of temperature in relation to body temperature. Does it feel hot or cold outside?

Talk about

Weather types, temperature in relation to the body, hot, cold, warm.

Weather chart

Objectives

Science: observing and recording changes in the weather.
Maths: considering time and the days of the week.

What you need

String, small pegs, card, felt-tipped pens.

What to do

Mount a length of string across a wall. Discuss the weather with the children daily, after outdoor play. On a piece of card, draw a sketch that represents the weather, and pin the card on the string. Discuss the previous day's weather and ask the children to forecast the following day's weather. Review the weather at the end of the week. Which day was the coldest? Which was the warmest?

Talk about

Weather types, days of the week, yesterday, tomorrow, today.

Weather words

Objectives

English: practising speaking and listening. Reading and writing with the teacher as scribe.

What you need

A large magnetic board and packet of small adhesive magnets, pieces of thin card, felt-tipped pens.

What to do

Encourage children to describe the day's weather, and write their words on the pieces of card. Fasten a magnet to the back of each card, and stick them on the board. Introduce new words where appropriate and write these down. Try using pens of different colours, varying the style of writing. Add some picture clues, for example, sketches of puddles or clouds. Read these cards with the children. The cards can be kept and added to on another occasion.

Leave the board in the writing area to encourage children to write their own words. Help them to fasten the magnets on to the cards.

Talk about

Types of weather, for example, rain, shower, drizzle, downpour.

Follow-up

English

Introduce familiar metaphors such as 'raining cats and dogs', and invite children to make up their own. My children suggested 'raining snails and slugs', because there were so many on the path outside after a shower.

I hear thunder

Objective

English: speaking and listening.

What you need

A cassette recorder and cassettes, headphones.

What to do

Many children find it comforting to talk about thunder and lightning and sing this rhyme in stormy weather:

I hear thunder, I hear thunder,
Yes, I do. Yes, I do.
Pitter-patter raindrops, pitter-patter
raindrops,
I'm wet through –
So are you.

As the children sing, record their song on a cassette. All the children's favourite songs and rhymes can be taped in this way. Put the cassettes in the listening centre for individual children to listen to and join in with the songs.

Talk about

Cassette player, making a cassette, recording, playing back, singing, listening.

Follow-up

English

Write the words to the children's favourite rhymes on cards, using the rebus technique (replacing some of the words with pictures). Place these cards by the listening centre to encourage reading behaviour.

Rainbow

Objective

Science: exploring light and colour.

What you need

Water, oil, a bowl or water tray.

What to do

With the children, look for a rainbow in the sky after a storm. On sunny days, they could look for a rainbow where the sun strikes the water tray or a glass.

Pour a little oil on the water in the bowl or tray. Place this in the sun and let the children watch for rainbows.

Talk about

Sunlight, rainbow, colour names.

Follow-up

Science

Encourage the children to make a rainbow using collage materials. Tissue paper, coloured film and thin fabrics are effective. The colours of the rainbow appear in the following order, from top to bottom: red, orange, yellow, green, blue, indigo and violet.

Bubbles

Objectives

Science: observing the direction and force of the wind.
Maths: considering shape and size.

What you need

Strong wire, a strong solution of washing-up liquid and water.

What to do

Twist the wire to make bubble-blowers of different sizes and shapes. Let the children dip these into the liquid and blow bubbles in the garden. Encourage them to observe whether the bubbles are carried away swiftly by the wind or whether they slowly rise and fall.

Discuss the direction in which the bubbles go, for example, towards the gate. Introduce the compass points north, south, east and west. This is most effective if the compass points are painted or chalked on the play surface.

Talk about

Wind direction and speed, compass points, bubble size, shape and height.

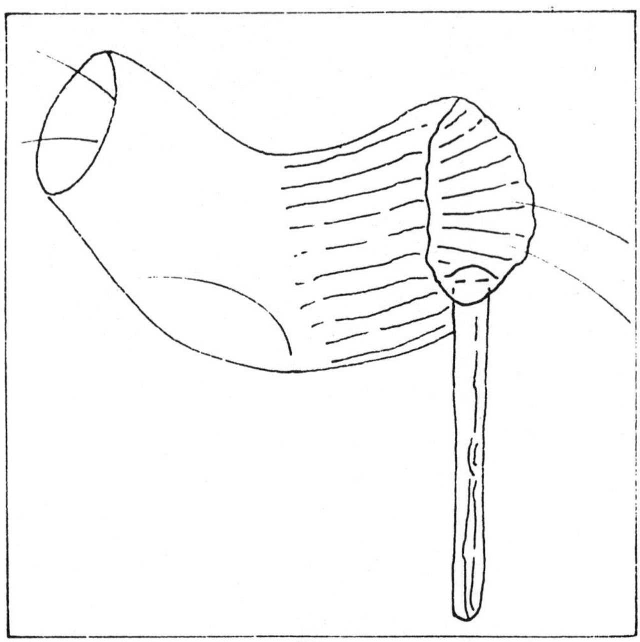

A wind-sock

Objective

Science: observing the direction of the wind.

What you need

An old lightweight sock with the toe cut out, a stick, a stapler.

What to do

Staple one side of the sock over the end of the stick, and take it outside on a windy day. Ask the children from which direction the wind is blowing. What else is blowing in the wind? Perhaps the children's scarves, hair and coats are flapping in the wind. Look together at the trees and bushes.

Take the wind-sock outside on a calm day and let the children see the difference between calm and windy conditions.

Talk about

Windy days, strong, calm, the effects of wind on clothes, trees and litter.

Weather vane

Objective

Science and technology: designing and making with a variety of materials.

What you need

A variety of materials to make streamers, including fabrics such as cotton and net, plastic sheeting, crêpe paper, newsprint and tissue paper, a range of holders including wood, twigs, drinking straws, tubes and thin plastic trays, a choice of fastenings such as paper-clips, a small stapler, PVA adhesive, a hole punch and thread.

What to do

Let the children choose some material for the streamer. Discuss with them the possibilities of the different materials and their attributes. Help them to cut a long thin streamer from the material. Then the children can choose a holder. Discuss the different types of fasteners together, and let the children choose one. They can then fasten the streamer to its holder. They may use several streamers on one holder if they wish.

Take the streamers outdoors and let the children watch as they blow in the wind. Can they tell which way the wind is blowing? Encourage them to compare a windy day with a calm day. Inside the nursery, discuss which streamers, holders and fasteners were the most effective and robust.

Talk about

Which material? Which holder? How? Does it work? What else can we try? How well did it work? How can we make a better one?

Follow-up

Science and technology

Let the children design and make a flag using similar materials but a different shape. Test the flags outdoors.

Science

With the children, fly a commercially-made kite. Discuss how to get it airborne. Why does it fall?

Windmill

Objective
Science: observing the direction and speed of the wind.

What you need
A windmill, either bought or home-made using paper, a pin, a stick and two beads.

What to do
If you are making a windmill, cut a square of paper. Fold alternate corners into the centre as shown in the diagram, and pin the windmill on the stick, with a bead on top of and underneath the paper to allow it to turn freely. It is important to supervise children's play with the windmill to ensure that the pin is not removed.

Windmills give children the opportunity to observe the speed of the wind. They respond to a breeze as well as to a strong wind. Ask the children how fast the windmill goes round. In which direction do they have to turn the windmill to make it spin? Why does it not spin in the other direction? What is making it go round? Is there a slight breeze or a strong wind? Can we make the windmill spin indoors? How? Ask the children to try blowing on the windmill, first softly and then hard. How long can they blow on the windmill before they run out of breath?

Talk about
Windmill, spin, slowly, fast, wind, breeze, strong, gale, blow, a long time, a short time, air, breath.

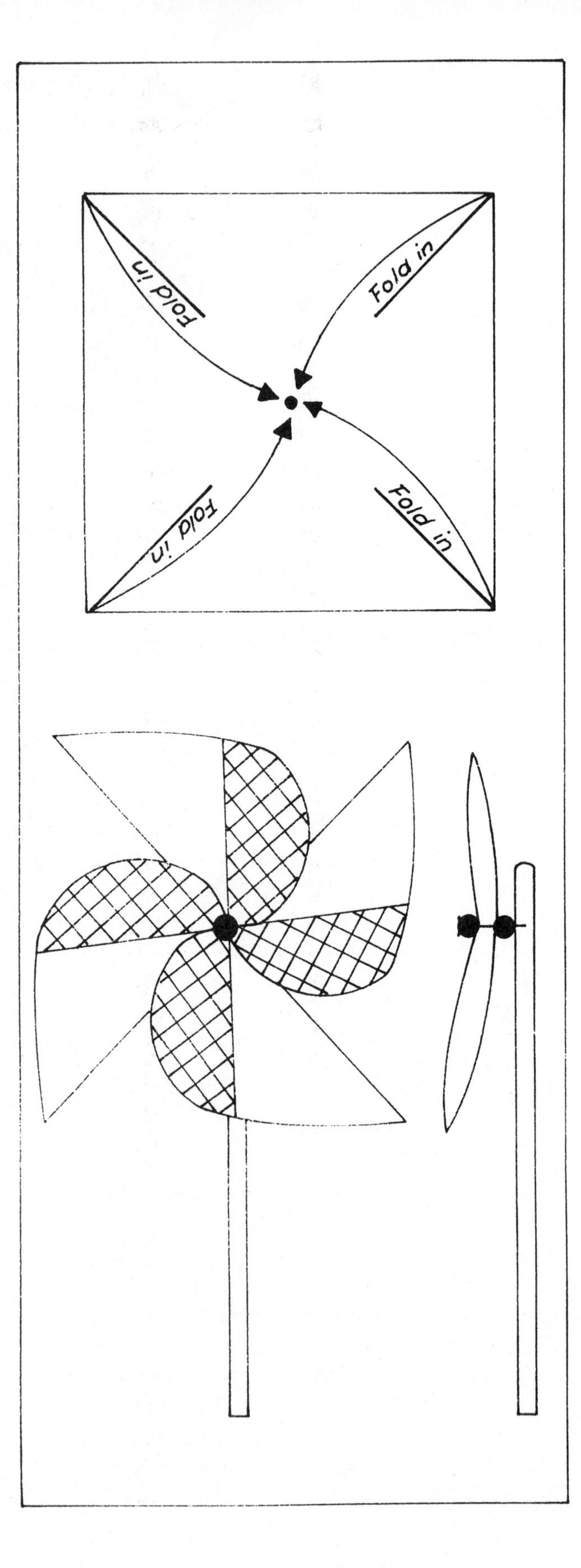

Let's meet a musician

Objective
Science: observing that sounds are made in a variety of ways.

What you need
A visit from a musician.

What to do
Invite a parent or an older child to play a wind instrument while the children listen. Ask the player to demonstrate how the instrument works and how different notes are made.

Talk about
Instrument, blow, air, notes, music.

Follow-up
Science
Introduce other instruments, and make a collection of instruments for the children to use.
Technology
Help the children to design and make instruments that can be blown, banged and shaken.

Boiling and freezing

Objective

Science: observing the properties of materials, in particular solids, liquids and gases.

What you need

A see-through saucepan with a lid, drinking water, dried soup mix, fruit juice, an ice-cube tray, cups, access to a cooker and a refrigerator with a freezing compartment.

What to do

On a cold day, add the required amount of water to a packet of dried soup mix. Taking the necessary safety precautions, an adult can boil the soup in a see-through pan so that the children can watch as the liquid boils and steam forms. At the end, remove the pan lid and let the children look at the drops of water that have formed on it. When the soup cools, serve it in cups and let the children taste it.

On a hot day, mix some water with the fruit juice and pour it into the ice-cube tray. Place the tray in the freezer. When the fruit ice-cubes are frozen, crush them and serve in cups as fruit slush.

Talk about

Water, dissolve, liquid, boil, steam, drops of water, evaporate, solid, freeze, ice, cold, warm, keeping cool, keeping warm.

Puddles

Objective

Science: observing the effects of the weather.

What you need

Tape or chalk.

What to do

On a rainy day, inside the nursery, let the children watch the pattern of rain as it finds a path down the windows and listen as it beats on the roof. When the rain stops, go out together to observe the changes. How many puddles are there? Tape or chalk round a puddle to indicate its present size. Return later with the children to note any changes.

If the sun comes out, the children can watch as the puddle gets smaller, but they will be equally delighted if the rain continues and it gets bigger. At the end of the session, take another measurement. Compare this with the size of the puddle the next day.

Talk about

Rain, puddle, number, comparative size, gets smaller, evaporates, gets bigger.

Follow-up

Maths

As children push wheeled toys through shallow puddles, encourage them to observe the parallel tracks made.

Science

Let the children use old paintbrushes to cover the paths with water, and watch as it evaporates in the sun.

Plumbing

Objectives

Science and technology: considering the properties of water and the types and uses of materials.

What you need

Plastic guttering, plumbing pipes and joints, a water tray.

What to do

Look at the sources of water in the nursery. Ask the children how they think it travels to the taps. Where do they think it goes? Look at the guttering outside, and ask them where the rain goes. How does it reach the drain?

Introduce some plastic guttering, plumbing pipes and joints to the water tray. Encourage the children to join these in different ways and pour water into them.

Talk about

Water, its passage and flow, pipes, shape, material.

Follow-up

Science

To encourage the children to investigate forces in relation to water, put squeezy washing-up liquid bottles in the water tray with empty soap or hand-cream dispensers which have pumps. Let the children explore how these work.

Doing the washing

Objective

Science: observing the effects of the weather in a familiar domestic context.

What you need

Unclaimed gloves or similar items from the lost property box, bowl, water, washing line and pegs.

What to do

Invite the children to wash the gloves and wring them out by hand. Ask the children where would be a good place to dry them. Try several places, including:

- the washing line outside;
- a cool cupboard;
- close to a source of heat, for example, a radiator.

Do not introduce too many variables, as it can confuse children.

Talk about

Dry, wet, hang up, lie flat, wind, sun, air, evaporate, drip.

Follow-up

Science

Introduce different materials to mop up water spills, such as a sponge, a cloth, newspaper, card and a plastic sheet. Ask the children which ones are most effective and why. Discuss absorbency.

Let's discover clothes

Objective
Science: considering the types and uses of materials.

What you need
Clothes suitable for different weather conditions and occasions.

What to do
With the children, discuss the different functions of clothes:
- to keep us dry (umbrellas, hoods and raincoats);
- to keep us warm (hats, scarves and gloves);
- to keep us cool (sunhats, shorts and tee-shirts).

Let them look at the different sorts of clothing and try them on.

Talk about
Weather types, keeping cool, warm, dry, names and attributes of clothes, for example, fleecy, waterproof.

Follow-up
Science
Together with the children, make a collection of shoes suitable for different sorts of weather, for example, boots, sandals and outdoor shoes.

Keeping dry

Objectives
Science: thinking about the types and uses of materials, and investigating waterproof materials.

What you need
An empty water tray, a watering can or empty washing-up liquid bottle, a doll, card, a stapler, scissors, a range of different fabrics, plastic sheeting.

What to do
Make a large card frame for each type of material, and staple the material to the card to make an 'umbrella'. Put the doll in the empty water tray. Place the umbrella over his head. Using a small watering can or washing-up liquid bottle, the children can make it 'rain' gently over the umbrella. They should gradually increase

the flow of water and watch what happens. Then they can repeat the experiment with the other fabric and plastic umbrellas.

Talk about

Water, rain, keeping dry, wet, soaking wet, umbrella, waterproof, not waterproof, names of fabrics.

What shall I wear?

Objective

English: speaking and listening.

What you need

Card, transparent self-adhesive plastic, felt-tipped pens.

What to do

Cut six pieces of card and draw an outline of a figure on each. Around each figure, draw symbols to show a specific sort of weather, such as raindrops, a sun, a snowman or a kite, or symbols to represent an occasion that requires particular clothes, such as bedtime or swimming. Draw clothes and accessories to match each card and fit the figure, for example, a raincoat, hat, boots and umbrella for the card with the raindrops.

Play a matching game in a non-competitive way, with the children sorting and discussing the clothes they are choosing to match their card. Encourage the children to help each other.

Talk about

Weather, clothes, taking turns.

Summer

Fine summer weather brings the opportunity for more outdoor exploration and activities. There is time to observe and investigate the minibeasts that live under stones, on leaves or in crevices of walls. The seashore introduces a different environment with more creatures, plants and materials to explore, and activities that extend sand and water play.

A walk round the nursery or school heightens children's awareness of familiar people and places. At the same time, children remember the events of the past year at nursery and look forward to the next.

The topics for summer are: 'Minibeasts', 'The seashore' and 'Our nursery'.

Minibeasts

Chapter four

Young children are fascinated by the minibeasts that are so evident in summer. The world of the minibeast is a doorstep jungle ready for exploration.

This topic provides the opportunity to introduce environmental issues concerning the welfare of wildlife. The collection of minibeasts must be supervised carefully, and minibeasts must be kept in an environment that caters for their needs. After observation, they must always be returned to their habitat.

Attitudes towards minibeasts such as spiders should be discussed in advance to ensure that they are positive. Invite the co-operation of parents in helping children to appreciate the wonders of the insect world.

Let's look for minibeasts

Objective

Science: watching minibeasts in their natural habitat.

What you need

Large magnifying glasses.

What to do

Before setting out to look for minibeasts, emphasise that children must not touch or move the minibeasts, but should inform staff so that everyone can watch them in their natural habitat.

Visit the garden or park to look for minibeasts. It is useful to have large magnifying glasses with which the children can observe them in location. As they find the creatures, discuss them, considering the following questions:

- What is the minibeast's colour? Does it have a pattern or markings (for example, the symmetry of a butterfly's wings)?
- What are its physical attributes? For example, does it have legs, wings or a shell?
- How does the minibeast move? Does it fly, crawl or slide?
- Where does it live? Under a stone, on a bush or in a flower?
- What does it eat?

Go out to look for minibeasts several times, until the children become familiar with observing minibeasts in their habitats and have been introduced to different species. Discuss the weather conditions. Which minibeasts appear in the sun? Which are evident after a shower of rain? How well do they camouflage themselves?

It is important that there is no collection of minibeasts for the first few observations, to ensure that children do not associate looking at minibeasts with collecting them. They should understand that it is better to observe animals in their habitat than through indiscriminate collection.

Collecting minibeasts

Objective

Science: developing an awareness of the sensitive collection and care of living things.

What you need

A prepared minibeast environment that reflects the needs of the species (see pages 61 to 63), a temporary container with air holes.

What to do

Before collecting minibeasts, let the children observe them in their habitat. Talk about what they eat, where they live, and what you will need to make a suitable environment for them.

Talk about

Minibeasts, colour, pattern, spots, stripes, wings, antennae, movement, fly, crawl, habitat.

Follow-up

Science

Visit a butterfly farm to observe the variety of butterflies and find out about their life-cycle.

When collecting minibeasts, it is important always to collect a few specimens only, keep them for a short period of time and then return them to their habitat. Never collect a protected species, and never collect butterflies, as they are easily damaged.

Before setting out, explain to the children that they should handle minibeasts as little as possible, because they are delicate and can easily be harmed. Ensure that the children know how many minibeasts they are to collect, and of which species, but do not discourage them from looking at and discussing other minibeasts in their habitat.

Ask children to inform staff when they find a minibeast, so that the transfer to the collecting jar is supervised and only the required number are collected.

Place the minibeast in its new home as soon as possible. Encourage the children to watch where it goes and how it moves. Ensure that there is an adequate supply of fresh suitable food.

Talk about

Minibeasts, collecting, taking care, food, looking after.

Follow-up

Maths

Make a map of the garden featuring familiar locations such as the sand pit and climbing frame. Let the children draw a picture of where each minibeast was collected, so that it can be returned to the same spot after observation.

Where was it found?

Objectives

Science: observing and recording the variety of life.
Maths: practising number and sorting according to different categories.

What you need

A large teacher-drawn colour picture featuring soil, grass, a plant with leaves, a wall and a stone, felt-tipped pens.

What to do

When the children have observed minibeasts in the garden, ask where they discovered them. Using a dark felt-tipped pen, draw on an outline of the minibeast, for example, a snail or spider, in the appropriate place on the pictorial chart. Count how many spiders have been found on the stone and how many on the wall. How many altogether?

Talk about

Places where minibeasts are found. How many? How many altogether?

Tell me

Objective

English: writing with the teacher as scribe.

What you need

Paper, felt-tipped pens, pencils and crayons.

What to do

Ask children to describe a minibeast they have found. Encourage them to tell you about:

- its name and what it looks like;
- where they found it and any incident relating to the find.

Write this information on the paper using the children's own words, to establish a link between speaking and writing. Read out the completed description, encouraging the children to participate. Encourage the children to crayon or draw letter shapes on the paper.

Talk about

Speaking, writing, reading, words, letters, letter sounds.

A minibeast jungle

Objective

Science: observing that minibeasts need certain conditions to sustain life.

What you need

A patch of garden and gardening tools.

What to do

This is a long-term project which can be started in spring when growing seeds (see Chapter 1, 'Growth'). The children can decide which minibeasts they wish to attract, help with preparing the habitat and then return at intervals to observe which minibeasts have settled in the area. Other groups of children can add new features to the minibeast jungle.

Some ideas for environments include:

- large stones, rotting logs and leaf litter for woodlice, beetles, worms and snails;
- buddleia for butterflies;
- long grass and plants prone to aphids to attract ladybirds;
- cabbages for white butterflies;
- evergreen ground- and wall-covering plants such as ivy to give shelter to spiders, silverfish and ants.

To undertake a short-term project, lay an old piece of sacking or large stone on a patch of garden. This will attract woodlice, slugs and spiders.

Talk about

Minibeasts, where they live and what they need to sustain life.

Let's discover snails

Objective

Science: observing and looking after invertebrates.

What you need

A transparent plastic tank such as a fish tank, a perforated lid or netting, damp soil, grass and other seeds, large stones, fresh green leaves, snails.

What to do

Set up the snails' habitat by placing a layer of damp soil at the bottom of the fish tank where the snails can lay their eggs. Grass and other perennials can be planted in the soil to give shade, and large stones will give shelter to the snails.

Place the tank where it is cool and shady, and put the snails in the prepared habitat with some fresh green leaves. Replace these each morning, as snails feed at night and the old leaves deteriorate rapidly.

Sprinkle the soil with water daily to keep the tank moist, otherwise the snails will become inactive. Clean the tank when required and search in the soil for eggs. The snails can be kept for up to five days.

Talk about

Snails, how they move, where they live, what they eat, looking after them.

How many snails?

Objective

Maths: recording number.

What you need

The class observation tank of minibeasts such as snails, paper, clipboard, pencils.

What to do

Invite the children to record the number of snails in the tank using the pencil and paper. The way in which they do this will indicate their understanding of number. Some children will draw a picture of each item, for example, a snail shape for each snail; others will draw a line or other tally to stand for each snail; and others will write the number sign.

Talk about

How many? Recording number, number names and signs.

Let's discover ladybirds

Objective

Science: observing and looking after ladybirds.

What do you need

A container such as a transparent tank, with sufficient room for the ladybirds to fly, netting, soil, stones, small plants, aphid-infested leaves and flowers, for example, beans and roses.

What to do

Put a layer of soil in the tank, and add some stones and small plants to give a garden-like environment. The infested leaves and flowers will provide the ladybirds with a source of aphids for food.

Place the ladybirds in the prepared tank with the food source, and cover the tank securely with netting. Encourage the children to compare the ladybirds for colour, size and number of spots. Ask the children how the ladybirds move, and how many legs they have. Let the children watch as they unfold their wings to fly, and observe as they feed on the aphids. The ladybirds can be kept for up to five days.

Talk about

Ladybirds and other beetles, how they move, what they eat.

Follow-up

Science

- Woodlice can be kept in a similar environment, with stones and bark for shelter. Keep the soil damp and feed the woodlice on rotting vegetables.
- Caterpillars can also be kept in an environment like this, but be sure to include a container of water with a fresh supply of the appropriate food plant. For example, the peacock and small tortoiseshell require stinging nettles, while the large and small white need cabbage leaves. Some caterpillars pupate on their food plant and others in the soil. Release the butterflies near nectar plants such as buddleia and clover shortly after they emerge from the chrysalis.

Let's discover spiders

Objective

Science: observing and looking after spiders.

What you need

A transparent plastic tank with sufficient space to build a web, netting, soil, twigs, a dish of water, some small live flies if possible.

What to do

Put a layer of soil in the bottom of the tank, and add some twigs to act as supports for web-building. Add a dish of water. Most spiders can survive for a short period without food, but it is desirable to introduce some small live flies into the tank as well. Spiders can be kept for up to five days.

The children can watch as the spider builds a web. Can they see which parts are built first? Encourage them to look at the pattern of the web and the strong sticky thread. Why do the children think the spider builds a web? Ask them to count the spider's legs, and observe as it moves over the twigs and soil. Can they see the spider waiting at the edge of the web? What is it doing? Why?

Talk about

Spiders, what they eat, how they move, where they live, how they catch flies.

Anansi

Objective

English: listening and responding to a story.

What you need

A story about Anansi, a cassette player with two or more sets of headphones, a cassette.

What to do

Stories about Anansi the spider-man come from West Africa and the Caribbean. Anansi, a mischievous character who outwits those around him, has much in common with Brer Rabbit.

These folk tales vary in format. Some are explanations of natural phenomena, for example, the reason for the elephant's trunk. Others are intended to instruct, in the manner of Aesop, developing an insight into vanity and other foibles. Whatever their content, the tales certainly entertain, and they give young children an opportunity to enjoy stories from a non-European culture.

Tell a story about Anansi to the children. Many of the stories feature repeated rhythmic phrases that are popular with children, inviting their participation and giving a sense of pattern. If you have a listening centre, record these stories on a cassette for the children to use. This encourages familiarity with well-known tales. As children listen to the tape, they can be heard joining in with the extracts they recognise.

Talk about

Anansi, stories, what happens next? Sounds and rhythms of language.

Follow-up

English

- Let the children write some of their favourite stories, with the teacher as scribe. Record these stories on cassette, and leave the stories beside the listening centre for children to refer to as they listen, encouraging reading behaviour.
- A selection of Anansi stories feature in the following books: *Anancy – Spiderman* by James Berry (Walker); *Listen to this Story* by Grace Hallworth (Methuen); and *Further Adventures of Brer Anansi* by David P. Makhanhall (Blackie). Be prepared to adapt these for telling to young children. A picture story book about Anansi is *A Story, A Story* by Gail E. Haley (Methuen).

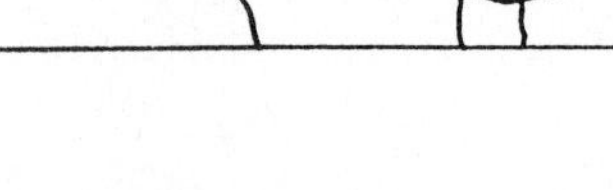

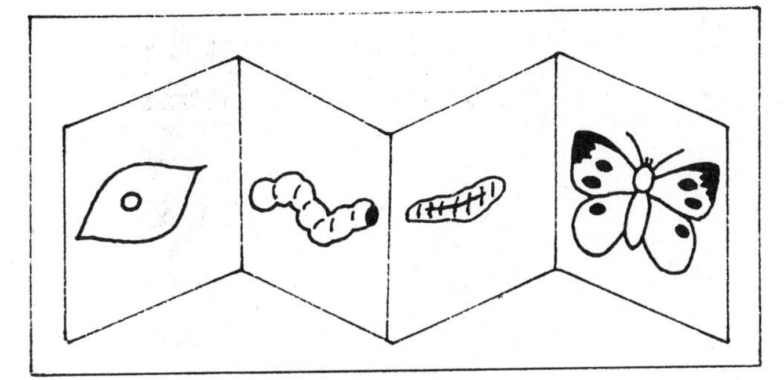

Mini-books

Objectives

Maths: sequencing the life-cycle of minibeasts.
English: writing for a purpose.

What you need

Sheets of card, felt-tipped pens.

What to do

Fold a strip of card into a zigzag book, and draw a picture of one stage of the life-cycle of a minibeast, such as a caterpillar, on each page of the book. Draw the life-cycle in sequence, from left to right.

Invite the children to suggest captions for the book. Write these down, and then read the book with the children.

Talk about

Time, first, next, and then, stages in the life-cycle.

Follow-up

Maths and science
Depict the stages of the minibeast's life in a recurring cyclical format (see 'Dandelion clock', page 17).
English
Provide zigzag folded paper in the writing area for children to make their own mini-books.

Observational painting

Objectives

Science: observing and recording.

What you need

Powder paint in tubs, a sponge, paintbrushes of different thicknesses, a pot of water, a palette, a minibeast in a prepared transparent container, a magnifying glass.

What to do

Invite children to observe and describe the minibeast, which might be a snail or a caterpillar. Discuss with them the shape, colour and size of the minibeast, and introduce the names of body parts.

The children can mix colours on the palette and use these to paint a picture of the minibeast. As they work, listen carefully to what children say they are seeing and drawing.

Talk about

Observing the minibeast closely, colour, size, shape, movement, body parts.

On the move

Objective

Maths: investigating shape, size, direction and speed.

What you need

A hall or large grassed area.

What to do

Use children's observations of minibeasts as a starting point for movement. For example, they could:

- make long, thin shapes like a caterpillar or worm;
- go down on all-fours like a spider;
- curl up like a snail in its shell;
- stand upright and with arms held wide to represent a butterfly.

In these shapes the children can move at the appropriate speed, for example, with long slow stretches for the worm and light quick steps for the butterfly. They can also vary the direction of movement, moving forwards, backwards and sideways in a spider shape, or up and down in a butterfly shape.

Talk about

Shape, size, direction and speed.

Minibeast mobile

Objective
Science and technology: designing and making a mobile using a variety of materials.

What you need
String, an assortment of boxes, tubes, fabric and paper, sticky tape, PVA adhesive, paper-clips, thread, hole punch, coat-hanger.

What to do
Invite the children to design and make a model of a minibeast of their choice. Offer them an assortment of materials and fasteners and talk with them as they make their model, actively encouraging purposeful choice and assisting them to accomplish their plans.

Cardboard tubes can be painted or covered in paper to represent bees and other flying insects. Coloured tissue and transparent paper can be overlaid to make butterfly wings. Strips may be cut from an egg box to make caterpillars; the children can cover them with a pattern using sequins and other small items. Follow the children's own ideas and suggestions.

Fix a long piece of string across the classroom and tie on the models to make a mobile. Smaller mobiles can be made by hanging the minibeast models from a coat-hanger.

Talk about
What does it look like? What can we use? How can we fasten it?

Modelling minibeasts

Objective
Maths: learning about shape and space.

What you need
Dough or clay.

What to do
Encourage the children to make minibeast shapes using a fixed quantity of dough or clay. Discuss the long thin worm shapes and short fat slug shapes that are formed. Encourage the children to curl worm shapes to make spiral snail shells.

Talk about
Same amount, different shapes, long and thin, short and fat, flat, spherical, spiral.

Follow-up
Maths
Offer the children circles of paper to cut into spirals. Attach a thread to the centre of each spiral and hang them up as a mobile. The children could use poster paper with a different colour on each side for an effective display.

Making faces

Objective
Maths: observing pattern and symmetry.

What you need
Face paints, a large unbreakable mirror.

What to do
Invite the children to paint their faces. Encourage them to look in the mirror and paint the same shape on each side of their face, for example, a cross on each cheek.

The children may choose to copy the patterns on a minibeast, such as a ladybird or butterfly.

Talk about
Pattern, symmetry, reflection.

Maxi-books

Objective

English: encouraging reading behaviour.

What you need

A large sheet of card, several sheets of thick paper, felt-tipped pens, carpet tape, thread, a strong needle.

What to do

Share some songs and action rhymes together, for example:

Incy Wincy Spider
Climbed up the spout,
Down came the rain and washed the spider out,
Out came the sunshine and dried up all the rain,
Incy Wincy Spider climbed up the spout again.

To make a maxi-book, fold the sheets of paper in half. Write a separate phrase of the rhyme on each page in large clear print. As you write, invite the children's questions about writing. Ask them to predict what you will write next. Illustrate each page, giving picture clues for the content.

Fold a sheet of card to make the cover, and write the title on it. Sew the book down the centre fold, and secure it with carpet tape.

Read the book with the children, pointing to the words to demonstrate the left-right orientation of print. Leave the book in the book corner to encourage reading behaviour.

Talk about

Writing, drawing, letters, words, reading stories and rhymes.

Honey tarts

Objective
Maths: measuring with standard units.

What you need
225g flour, 100g margarine, water, a pot of honey, a bowl, a fork, several small rolling pins, pastry cutters, a bun tin, an oven.

What to do
Honey is the product of bees' summer activity. Using honey in the food area gives children the opportunity to taste it and talk about the bees that made it.

Measure out the flour, and rub in the margarine with your fingers. Add a little water, and mix with a fork to give a soft dough. Give each child a piece of dough and a small rolling pin, and let them roll out the dough. Then they can cut out shapes with the pastry cutters, and place the pastry in the bun tin. Fill each tart with a spoonful of honey, and bake them in the oven at 200°C, 400°F or gas mark 6 for 15 to 20 minutes until golden brown.

Talk about
Measures, ingredients, honey and how bees make it, the effects of heat.

Follow-up
Maths
Make honey sandwiches to eat at a teddy bears' picnic. Invite children and parents to bring their bears. The children can compare the bears for colour, size and features, and look for patterns in the bears' clothes or fur.

The seashore

Chapter five

The seashore brings a wealth of enjoyable experiences and a new environment to explore. The sand and water that seem so familiar in the nursery take on new dimensions as children observe them closely and use them as a basis for many activities. Shells and pebbles provide material for sorting, matching and pattern. If it is not possible to visit the beach, give children the seaside experience by putting shells and pebbles in the sand area.

During the summer many families plan to travel. Setting up a travel agency where children can plan and choose holidays brings the opportunity for worthwhile literacy activities.

Let's visit the seashore

Objective

Science: observing familiar materials in their natural setting.

What to do

A visit to the seashore with young children needs careful planning. Consult tide tables before setting a date. Check with the school and Local Authority to ensure that there is an adequate adult to child ratio and that recommended guidelines are followed.

At the beach, discourage indiscriminate collection of living creatures. It may be possible for samples to be brought back and kept in appropriate conditions.

Collect a variety of different shells, stones and seaweed to take back. Take back a bucketful of sand for close observation in the nursery.

Bring along the nursery sand equipment, including sieves, funnels, tubing and a sandwheel, for the children to use in a new context.

Take the children to visit a fish stall near the beach. Look at the display of sea creatures, including crabs and winkles. Encourage the children to take a deep breath, taking in the smells as well as the sights.

Talk about

Seashore, names of shells, sea creatures.

Sand activities

Objectives

Maths: exploring space and shape.
Science: finding out about the properties of sand.

What you need

A sandpit or a visit to the beach.

What to do

These activities are suitable for the beach or the sandpit. Projects of a larger scale can be encouraged at the beach, where children can plan and build together.

- Start a row of sand pies and invite everyone to add one. Use buckets of different shapes and sizes and compare the pies.
- Make a sandcastle together. The children can scoop sand on to the mound, pat it with their hands to make it firm and use shells and small stones to decorate it.
- Encourage the children to make patterns and pictures in the sand using shells, seaweed and pebbles.
- Show the children how to make marks and impressions in the sand with a finger or stick.

Talk about

Sand, wet, mould, make prints, patterns, names of shells and pebbles.

What is sand?

Objective

Science: investigating natural materials.

What you need

Beach sand, a sheet of black paper, a magnifying viewer, sieves of different gauges.

What to do

Spread some beach sand over the black paper and let the children look for tiny pieces of shell and pebble. Cut some black paper to fit the bottom of the magnifying viewer, and place this inside the viewer with some sand. What can the children see? What colours are the small stones? What else can they see?

Let the children sift beach sand through sieves of different gauges. Ask them to observe closely the pieces left in the sieve. What do they think these are? Where did they come from? Why are the pieces of shell and pebble so small? What is sand?

Talk about

Sand, shells, stones.

Follow-up

Science

Let the children observe pebbles and different grades of gravel and sand under a magnifying glass.

English

Encourage children to make marks in wet sand using their fingers, to encourage writing behaviour. Ask them to write their names.

What are shells?

Objective

Science: investigating natural materials.

What you need

A sea tank if available (see page 76). An information book with colour photographs of sea creatures, an assortment of seashells, for example, limpets, mussels, cockles, whelks, slippers and topshells. These may be alive in the sea tank or a collection of empty shells – it is useful to have both.

What to do

Encourage the children to look closely at the empty shells. Ask them to see if any of the shells fit together. What shape and colour are the shells? For which creatures do they provide a home? What are the shells called? What do they look like?

Encourage the children to refer to the colour photographs in the information book and to look at the creatures in the sea tank if you have one.

Ask the children why they think these creatures need a shell. How does it help to protect them? How do they stay on the rocks without being washed away by the sea? Let the children examine a winkle or other mollusc in the sea tank, and try to detach it from the side of the tank. What happens when they touch a limpet?

Talk about

Shells, sea creatures and their names.

Follow-up

Maths

Sort and match shells for shape, size and colour.

Pebbles

Objective

Science: investigating natural materials.

What you need

An assortment of pebbles from the beach, a dish of water, a magnifying glass.

What to do

Let the children hold the pebbles. How do they feel? Why are they so smooth when stones in the garden are rough? Listen to the children's ideas and discuss the action of the sea on the rocks, gradually smoothing the surface.

Ask the children to scratch the surface of the pebbles. Are some pebbles harder than others? Ask the children which pebbles seem hardest.

With the children, look at the different colours of the pebbles. Do any have attractive bands or other markings? There may be fossils in the rock, possibly seashells; if so, discuss how these were formed. Encourage the children to inspect the pebbles closely using the magnifying glass.

Let the children place some of the pebbles in the dish of water and observe the effect on the colours of the pebbles.

Talk about

Pebbles, dull, shiny, names of familiar local rock types, for example, chalk, sandstone and granite.

Water plants

Objective

Science: observing the variety of life.

What you need

Several types of seaweed or pondweed, including one that is attached to a piece of rock, a tank of water, white absorbent paper such as sugar paper or blotting paper.

What to do

The following investigation may be carried out with seaweed brought back from the beach or with freshwater pondweed which can be bought from pet shops. There are various different types of pondweed, for example, Canadian pondweed which roots in gravel, willow moss which attaches itself to rocks and duckweed which floats on the surface. The focus of the observation is how water plants are supported and take shape in water. Out of the water they become flaccid and shapeless.

Let the children observe the water plants, comparing them for colour and other features. Look for any lettuce-like and feathery plants. The children can place these in the tank of water and watch as they take shape.

If you have a piece of bladderwrack, let the children examine it and look at its air pockets. They can place the seaweed in the tank and watch as it floats. What do they think is helping the bladderwrack to float? Do any other seaweeds have a tough, leathery surface to help them withstand the sea and rocks?

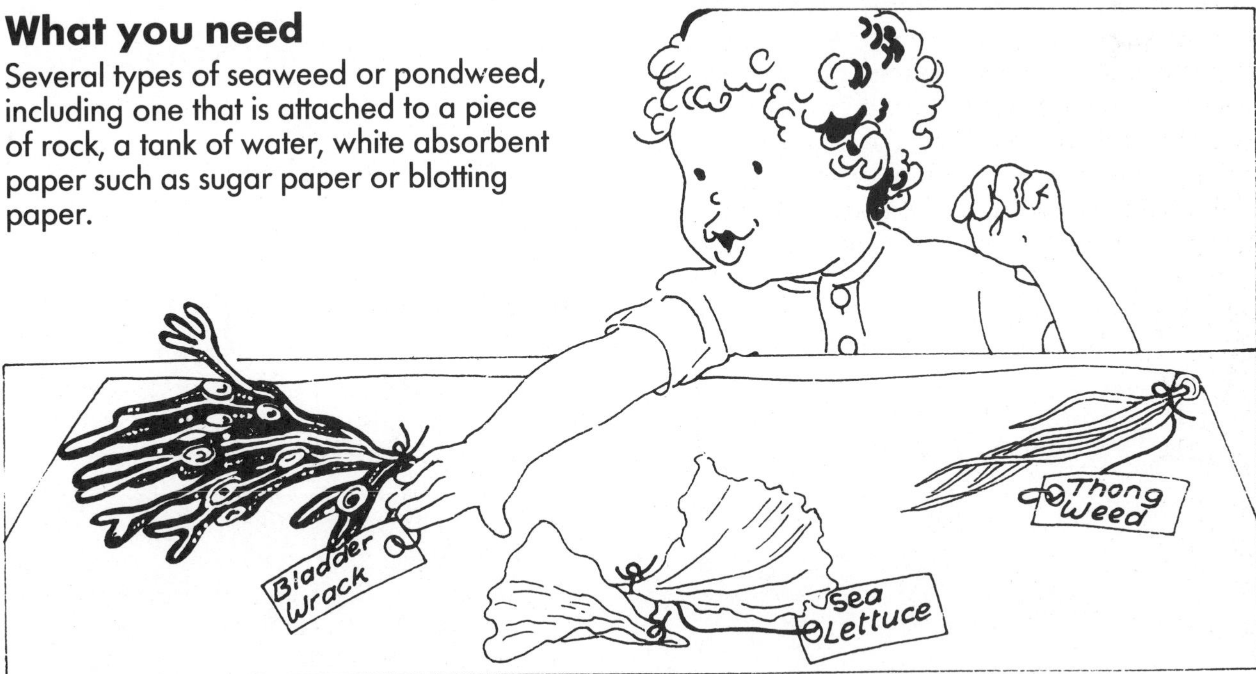

Look together at the way water plants attach themselves to rocks. Examine a strand of seaweed or pondweed that has rooted around a piece of rock or wood, and let the children observe the holdfast or root-like structure that clamps the plant to the surface.

Place some water plants on a piece of absorbent white paper to display their shape and colour.

Talk about

Seaweed, pondweed, names, parts, colours, texture, shape. What sorts of animals live in the shelter of water plants? Which species eat water plants?

Let's observe water creatures

Objective

Science: observing the variety of life.

What you need

A transparent plastic tank with a large water surface and a lid, an aerator.

For a marine tank: seawater, sand, gravel, rocks, seaweed of the feathery or lettuce type, a selection of sea creatures, for example, a sea-anemone, a small starfish, some winkles, limpets and mussels. Do not include crabs as they muddy the water. Keep marine animals no longer than five days. Transport seawater in large soft drinks containers with lids.

For a freshwater aquarium: gravel, oxygenating plants such as Canadian pondweed, water snails and goldfish, goldfish food. If tap water is used, it needs to stand in a bucket overnight. Goldfish can be kept indefinitely.

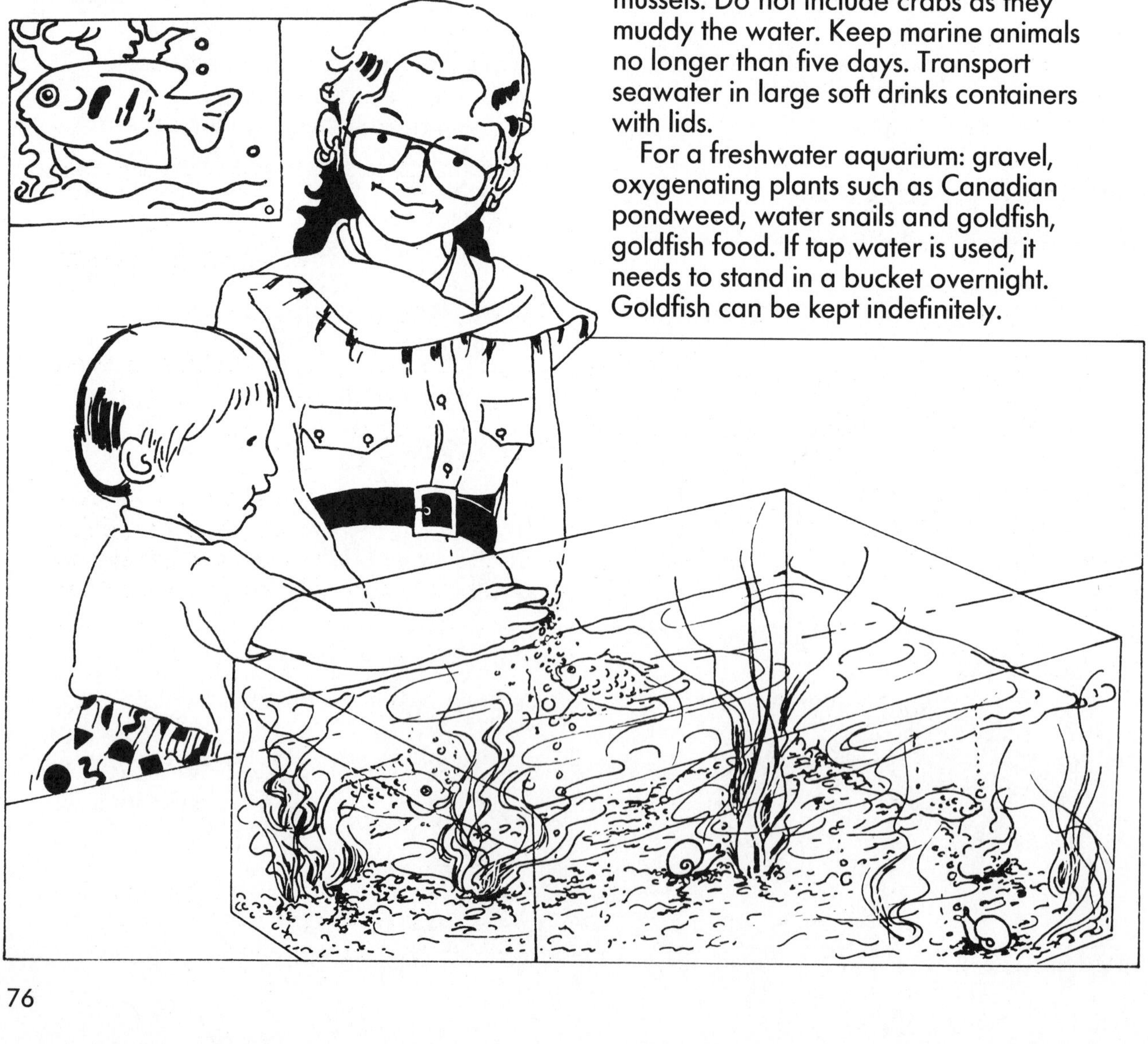

What to do

Encourage the children to observe the water creatures. How do they move? What do they look like? What do they eat? Look at the plants that live in water.

The children can feed goldfish, but this needs to be supervised to ensure that the fish are not overfed. Children can also help with cleaning the tank when this becomes necessary.

Talk about

Water creatures, names, where they live, how they move and what they eat.

Follow up

Science

Buy a whole fish from the fishmonger or supermarket for the children to observe, feel and name its parts.

Shell shapes

Objective

Maths: learning about shape and space.

What you need

A selection of shells and pebbles, a sand tray, wet and dry sand.

What to do

Add some shells and pebbles to the sand tray. Let the children use them as moulds and to make prints in wet sand; they can also be used for decorating sand pies. In dry sand, the children can use them for scoops and for making patterns.

Talk about

Shells, shape, size, print, pattern.

Follow-up

Science

Introduce some shells and pebbles to the water tray, and let the children find out whether they float or sink.

Shell boxes

Objective
Science and technology: designing and making using natural materials.

What you need
Small shells, small pebbles, PVA adhesive, card, margarine tubs with fitting lids.

What to do
Invite the children to make a shell picture or pattern. If they wish they can stick shells and pebbles on to margarine tubs with fitting lids to make shell boxes. Alternatively, they can use the card to make shell pictures.

Talk about
Shells, pebbles, colour, shape, pattern.

Shell prints

Objective
Maths: exploring shape and space.

What you need
Shells, including bivalve shells such as cockles, mussels and scallops, dough or clay.

What to do
Let the children use both sides of a bivalve to make prints and impressions in dough or clay. Encourage them to make prints with different parts of other shells, and compare the flat surfaces with the sharp pointed ones. Look together at any patterns formed by the shell texture.

These impressions can be left to dry and then varnished and displayed.

Talk about
Shells, texture, surface, smooth, rough, pattern, fit together.

Follow-up
Maths
The children could also make prints using fishing net, rope, twine and string.

Sand pictures

Objective

Science: investigating the types and uses of materials.

What you need

Sand, dark paper, PVA adhesive, brushes.

What to do

Invite the children to paint a picture using the PVA adhesive. Show them how to cover the picture with sand, and then shake off any excess to reveal the sand picture.

Talk about

Sand, adhesive, sticks, does not stick.

Water colours

Objective

Science: investigating the types and uses of materials.

What you need

A water tray and equipment, food colourings.

What to do

Encourage the children to look at objects both under the water and outside the water tray. Do they notice any differences in the way the objects look? Discuss transparency with the children.

Add some colouring to the water and let the children watch as it dissolves. What colour is the water now?

Discuss the uses of water for making drinks, watering the garden and washing. Can the children think of any other uses? Talk about the things we do in water, such as swim, bath, paddle, fish and sail.

Talk about

Water, transparency, dissolve.

Follow-up

Technology

Encourage the children to design and make a boat or floating object with scrap materials, and test it in the water tray.

Science

- Ask the children to look for other transparent objects, such as plastic trays, bottles and sweet papers.
- Invite the children to choose a flavour from a range of fruit squashes, and add water to dilute the squash. Discuss with the children the different flavours and colours, and the effect of adding water to the squash.

Catching fish

Objective
Maths: comparing objects for size.

What you need
A water tray, cones, gravel, shells and other small objects, netting of different gauges, for example, a piece of fishing net found on the shore, pieces of fruit and vegetable sacking, quoits, a needle, strong thread, sieves, strainers and colanders.

What to do
Fold a piece of netting over each quoit and sew it in place to make a fishing net. Leave one quoit without netting.

Put the strainers and nets in the water tray. Invite the children to use them to 'catch fish'. They will find that some objects go through the larger holes only. The finer nets will catch everything.

Introduce a quoit without any netting. Ask the children how many objects will pass through the quoit. How can they catch these objects? Which net do they think is the best for catching fish?

Talk about
How many? Too big, too small.

Follow-up
Technology
Invite the children to design and make 'fish' from foil, plastic, paper and other materials. What happens to paper fish when they have been in the water? Which materials are the best for making fish?

Maths
Sing the rhyme '1 2 3 4 5, once I caught a fish alive', using fingers to represent each number.

Fishing game

Objective
Science: using the senses to observe the variety of life.

What you need
A bag, seashore objects such as shells, pebbles, a feather, a crab claw, a net, a small crab shell, dried seaweed.

What to do
Put the seashore objects in a large bag. Invite one of the children to put her hand in the bag and feel one of the objects. Ask her to describe the shape and texture of the object, and guess what it might be. Then she can pull the object out to check. Ask the children to name and discuss the object.

At the end of the game sort the objects into categories agreed by the children, for example, things that feel smooth.

Talk about
Seashore objects, their shape, texture, size, attributes and names.

Travel agency

Objective

English: writing for a purpose.

What you need

Travel brochures, posters, forms, a telephone, memo pads, pens, pencils, a globe, maps, booking forms, used tickets.

What to do

Talk about visiting other places. Discuss the different ways of travelling – by train, coach, car and plane. Where would the children like to stay? At a friend's house, in a caravan, in a tent or at a hotel? Talk about local visits as well as more distant locations, so that all children can discuss their experiences of going to another place. What sorts of places have the children visited? Who has visited the seaside, farm, town or city? What did they see? Shops, animals, castles, mountains or lakes? Where would the children like to go? Look at the brochures together, and discuss different destinations.

Who would the children like to see when they go on holiday? Many children have relatives living in different areas, and they often associate a place with the people they meet. Introduce a globe and some maps. The children can look for the blue sea and the coloured land. Some children may wish you to locate places they have visited or have heard about.

Reorganise the writing centre to make a travel agency, introduce the brochures and display travel posters. Leave order forms, luggage labels, envelopes and paper on the desk. Place a memo pad and diary by the telephone. Talk about booking and paying for tickets.

Talk about

Travel agent, reading the brochure, checking the times, filling in forms, writing a letter, a memo and a diary.

Follow-up

Maths

Introduce the ideas of money, cheque books and bank cards.

Travel choices

Objective
Maths: recording number.

What you need
A clipboard and pencil, pictorial order forms.

What to do
Make some pictorial order forms like those shown here. One could be headed 'I want to visit . . . ', featuring the sea, a farm, mountains and a castle, and the other could say 'I want to travel by . . . ', with pictures of a plane, boat, train, car and bus.

Invite the children to use the order forms to survey how their friends wish to travel, and the type of holiday they want. Ask them to make a mark or tally beside the appropriate picture for each answer. Count the tallies together.

Talk about
How many? More than, the same number, less than, number names.

Follow-up
English
Invite children to write their name beside the holiday or vehicle of their choice.

Holiday time

Objective
English: speaking and listening.

What you need
A large box such as those used to protect machines for delivery, a suitcase, a book of road maps, unbreakable sunglasses, a sun hat, a bucket, a spade, picnic equipment.

What to do
Cut 'windows' in the large box to turn it into a vehicle. It is best if the type of vehicle is not defined; then children may use it as a plane, ship or car. Place the vehicle near the home corner.

Introduce the suitcase and other holiday items to the role-play area to stimulate children's imaginative play.

Talk about
Going on holiday, travelling, packing, reading a map.

Follow-up
English
Introduce used and unwanted postcards and pencils to encourage mark-making.

Our nursery

Chapter six

Summer brings the opportunity to explore the nursery grounds and vicinity, and to observe seasonal changes in trees, flowers and wildlife. Painting easels can be taken outside for children to record their observations.

Outdoor activities feature more prominently in the summer, and there are plenty of ideas for extending children's play with rhymes, songs and games. Introduce small equipment such as hoops so that children can explore shape and space as they enjoy the summer sun.

Many children will be preparing to transfer to a new school or class, and will need help and support to achieve this successfully. You can introduce children to the staff and new friends they will meet in their next school or class.

Walkabout

Objectives

Science: observing seasonal changes.
English: speaking and listening.
Maths: considering location and direction.

What you need

A camera.

What to do

Arrange to tour the nursery or a local primary school, to heighten children's awareness of their own environment or introduce a new one. Meeting people and visiting places helps children to settle into their present or future environments. Visits such as this are useful at different times to help the transitions from home to nursery and from nursery to school.

Visit the headteacher's office, the hall and other classes. Arrange for children to spend time in the class, usually Reception, that they will join in the near future. Introduce the staff and children. Take photographs of places and people.

Walk outside to take photographs from different angles, near and far, back and front. Look together at the building. Examine the materials used to make the walls, roof and windows. Look for shapes in the windows and doors, and patterns in the paving, fencing and brickwork.

Look for seasonal changes in the trees, flowers and wildlife. How tall are the seeds the children planted in the spring? How many birds can they see in the grounds?

Talk about

Nursery and school, names of rooms, people and outside areas, seasonal changes.

Follow-up

Science

- Go for a listening walk around the nursery. What sounds can the children hear inside? Listen for insects and birds outside.
- Look for machines that use electricity in school.

English

- Assemble the photographs with captions in a book depicting life at school.
- Invite Reception teachers to read a story to nursery children.

Do you remember?

Objective

Maths: considering time.

What you need

A nursery year book with photographs of shared events.

What to do

Together with the children, look at photographs and objects recalling the past year. Encourage the children to describe and sequence events they have enjoyed. Compare the nursery garden at different seasons. What clothes were the children wearing outside in winter? What clothes are they wearing now?

Talk about

Time, months, days, seasons.

Let's meet people who work at the nursery

Objective

English: speaking and listening.

What to do

Give the children a chance to meet the people working at the nursery or in their next school. Invite the caretaker, cleaner, cook, gardener, dinner supervisor and others to demonstrate and discuss their work. For example, you could visit the kitchen and watch the cook at work. What tools does the cook use? Discuss with the children any equipment the staff use to help them with their work.

How does the staff's work change over the year? The caretaker may be able to describe gritting the paths in winter and supervising decorators in the spring.

Talk about

People who work at the nursery or school, their names and jobs, the equipment used, seasonal changes.

Let's visit the office

Objectives

English: considering the uses of literacy.
Technology: learning about the functions of machines.

What to do

Visit the office of the nursery or a local primary school. It may be advisable to take children to visit the office in small groups. Introduce the secretary and talk about his or her work in the school.

If possible, look at the machines in the office. There may be a word processor, an electric typewriter and a photocopier. Arrange with the secretary in advance for a parent notice to be typed and photocopied while the children watch. Discuss the function of the machines with the children.

Ask the children what other ways there are of sending a message. Look for the telephone and postage stamps. Is there a fax machine? Make a phone call from the office to a volunteer parent.

Talk about

The secretary, machines and their function, making notices, sending messages.

Welcome

Objectives

English: writing for a purpose.
Technology: introducing the functions of machines.

What you need

Paper, pens, stapler, a photocopier, a typewriter or word processor if possible.

What to do

Invite children to talk about the experiences and activities that they have enjoyed in the nursery. Acting as scribe, you can type their words on the typewriter or word processor. Ask the children to illustrate their work and write messages of welcome to new entrants.

Let the children help you to photocopy the pages and assemble them into a 'Welcome' booklet for new children and their parents.

Talk about

Typing, writing, reading, making books, photocopy, print-out.

Crayon holder

Objective
Science and technology: designing and making with a variety of materials.

What you need
Scrap materials such as containers, tubes, firm boxes and washing-up liquid containers, coloured papers, PVA adhesive.

What to do
Invite children to design and make something for use in the nursery. Encourage them to make their own suggestions and try out their ideas. A crayon holder using a decorated container or flat tray is popular. An office tidy can be made by fixing tubes of different lengths together.

Talk about
What do we need? How can we make it? What can we use?

Milkshake

Objective
Science: investigating materials.

What you need
Milk, cups, handwhisk, milkshake mix of different flavours, for example, banana, strawberry and chocolate.

What to do
Invite children to choose a flavour of milkshake and whisk it with milk in a cup. Many children have milk daily at nursery, and it can be used for this activity, which presents a familiar drink in a new way, providing a focus for discussion and for the expansion of social skills.

Talk about
Milk, whisk, flavour names.

Follow-up
Science
Let the children watch as you make custard, observing the effect of heat as the liquid thickens.

Clapping games

Objective
Science: making sounds.

What to do
Clapping names is a way of introducing children to each other and making sure that they know each other's names. It ensures that children become acquainted with their nursery group.

Sit in a circle so that children can see each other easily. Ask each child to say his name for the whole group to clap. Clap the children's names in turn, giving one clap for each syllable. Clap your own name, too.

Introduce some of the different objects in the nursery and clap their names. Try to choose objects with a different number of syllables in their name, for example, pen, pencil, radio and television. This is a useful way of ensuring that children are familiar with the names of equipment.

Talk about
Clapping, how many? Names of nursery children, staff and objects.

Summer painting

Objective
Science: observing and recording.

What you need
Easels, paint and brushes.

What to do
Fine weather brings the opportunity to observe and record flowers and trees in the nursery grounds. Encourage the children to choose a part of the building or grounds to observe and paint.

Take the easels outside and place them near some flowers, perhaps the sunflowers children have grown. Invite the children to paint pictures of the flowers. Listen as children talk about what they are representing.

Talk about
Flowers and their parts, close observation, colours, shapes, insects that visit the flowers.

Playground games

Objective

English: speaking and listening.

What you need

An outside area.

What to do

Traditional playground games are a feature of nursery and school life. Staff and children can exchange games and rhymes. However, many children are not familiar with traditional games. Introduce a variety of playground games and skipping rhymes, including hopscotch and games such as 'What's the time, Mr. Wolf?'. Start with familiar ring games such as 'Ring o' roses' and 'Here we go round the mulberry bush'.

Paint some new floor markings on the outside play area to encourage children to make up their own games, for example, 'Hop on spots' and 'Follow my leader'.

Talk about

Traditional songs, rhymes and games.

This is the way

Objective
English: speaking and listening.

What to do
Sing the following rhyme, with the children doing suitable actions. The tune is 'Here we go round the mulberry bush'.

This is the way we walk to school, walk to school, walk to school,
This is the way we walk to school on a bright and sunny morning.

Vary the actions in subsequent verses to include jumping, skipping and hopping. You can also vary the weather, for example, 'This is the way we skate to school on a cold and icy morning', or 'This is the way we splash to school on a wet and rainy morning'.

Talk about
Rhymes, doing the actions, moving in different ways.

Acting rhymes

Objective
English: speaking and listening.

What you need
An outdoor area.

What to do
Traditional rhymes can be a good source of playground games. Sing their favourite rhymes with the children, and invite them to 'be' Humpty Dumpty or Jack and Jill. Props are not necessary, but sometimes children decide to use available outdoor equipment such as blocks to build Humpty Dumpty's wall.

Talk about
Singing rhymes, nursery rhyme characters.

Hoops

Objective
Maths: considering shape and space.

What you need
Plastic hoops of different sizes.

What to do
Sunny days enable children to play outside for longer periods. This gives them a chance to play in a large space where they can explore further ways of using nursery equipment. It also brings opportunities to experience the fresh air and physical activity essential for healthy growth.

Introduce a range of hoops to the outdoor play area. Encourage children to explore their shapes and uses. Here are some ideas:
- rolling a hoop to a partner and back;
- twisting hoops so that they revolve;
- placing a row of hoops on the ground and jumping from one to another.

Talk about
Hoops, shape, roll, turn.

Follow-up
Science
Encourage the children to make shadows with the hoops and other equipment, and to observe how the shadow changes when the object is turned.

Beanbags

Objective
Maths: considering shape, space and time.

What you need
Beanbags.

What to do
Introduce beanbags to outdoor play. Some ideas for using beanbags include:
- catching and throwing beanbags to a partner;
- catching and throwing a beanbag alone;
- placing a hoop on the ground and aiming to throw the beanbag into the hoop.

Talk about
Beanbags, catch, throw, land, inside the hoop, outside.

Bats and balls

Objective

Maths: considering shape, space and time.

What you need

Bats and balls of different sizes.

What to do

Introduce bats and balls of different sizes to the outdoor area. Some ideas include:

- rolling, bouncing and kicking balls to each other;
- catching and throwing balls with a partner;
- using bats with the balls.

Talk about

Balls, shape, size, catch, throw, bat, kick, roll, bounce.

Book list

Homes and families

Alex's Bed, Mary Dickinson (Hippo Books).
There's a Hippopotamus on Our Roof Eating Cake, Hazel Edwards (Hodder & Stoughton).
Doing the Washing, Sarah Garland (Picture Puffin).
Better Move on, Frog, Ron Maris (Collins).
Is anyone home?, Ron Maris (Walker Books).
My Book, Ron Maris (Picture Puffin).
Not Now, Bernard, David McKee (Sparrow).
Gran and Grandpa, Helen Oxenbury (Walker Books).
The New Baby, Kate Petty and Lisa Kopper (Franklin Watts).
On Friday Something Funny Happened, John Prater (Picture Puffin).
Janine and the New Baby, Iolette Thomas (Julia MacRae Books).
Noisy Nora, Rosemary Wells (Picture Lions).
Emma and the Vacuum Cleaner, Gunilla Wolde (Hodder & Stoughton).

Growth

Jim and the Beanstalk, Raymond Briggs (Picture Puffin).
Quack Quack, Patricia Casey (Walker Books).
Happy Birthday, Sam, Pat Hutchins (Picture Puffin).
Titch, Pat Hutchins (Picture Puffin).
You'll Soon Grow Into Them, Titch, Pat Hutchins (Picture Puffin).
In My Garden, Ron Maris (Walker Books).
Tom and Pippo in the Garden, Helen Oxenbury (Walker Books).
You Can't Catch Me, John Prater (Bodley Head).
Early Morning in the Barn, Nancy Tafuri (Picture Puffin).

Weather

Sally-Anne's Umbrella, Petronella Brienburg (Bodley Head).
Mog and Bunny, Judith Kerr (Collins).
Having a Picnic, Sarah Garland (Picture Puffin).
Mrs. Mopple's Washing Line, Anita Hewett (Picture Puffin).
Alfie's Feet, Shirley Hughes (Picture Lions).
The Wind Blew, Pat Hutchins (Picture Puffin).

Minibeasts

Anancy – Spiderman, James Berry (Walker Books).
Do You Want To Be My Friend?, Eric Carle (Picture Puffin).
The Very Busy Spider, Eric Carle (Hamish Hamilton).
The Very Hungry Caterpillar, Eric Carle (Hamish Hamilton).
Alex's Outing, Mary Dickinson (Hippo Books).
A Story, A Story, Gail E. Haley (Methuen Children's Books).
Listen to this Story, Grace Hallworth (Methuen Children's Books).
The Giant Jam Sandwich, John Vernon Lord (Piccolo).
Further Adventures of Brer Anansi, David P. Makhanhall (Blackie).
Winston's New Pet, Eileen Ryder (Burke Books).
Have You Seen The Crocodile?, Colin West (Walker Books).

The seashore

The Lighthouse Keeper's Lunch, Rhonda and David Armitage (Picture Puffin).
Four Brave Sailors, Mirra Ginsburg and Nancy Tafuri (Walker Books).
The Bears Who Went to the Seaside, Susanna Gretz (A & C Black).
Lucy and Tom at the Seaside, Shirley Hughes (Carousel).
A Day by the Sea, Joan Solomon (Hamish Hamilton).

Our nursery

Starting School, Janet and Alan Ahlberg (Viking Kestrel).
My Brother Sean, Petronella Brienburg (Bodley Head).
But Martin!, June Counsel (Corgi).
What's the Time, Mr. Wolf?, Colin Hawkins (Heinemann).
Spot Goes to School, Eric Hill (Heinemann).
Lucy and Tom Go to School, Shirley Hughes (Corgi).
On the Way Home, Jill Murphy (Picturemac).
Owl at School, Helen Nicoll and Jan Pienkowski (Picture Puffin).

Poetry and rhymes

Out and About, Shirley Hughes (Walker Books).
Five Furry Teddies, Linda Hammond (Puffin).

Resources

Here are some suggestions for resources for seasonal activities. They are grouped here under subject headings. However, children may use equipment freely as a source of manipulative, collaborative or imaginative play. Children will discover the types and uses of materials as they use them to create patterns or imaginative contexts.

Science

Investigating natural materials

Add the following to sand, water, clay and scrap materials:

- shells;
- pebbles;
- stones;
- fossils;
- leaves;
- twigs;
- pine-cones;
- conkers;
- feathers;
- wood.

Investigating living things

The following equipment will be useful:

- gardening equipment, including a trowel, fork, wheelbarrow and watering can;
- soil;
- seeds, including some from fruit, vegetables and flowers;
- bulbs;
- plant pots;
- an indoor propagator;
- a vase;
- magnifying viewers;
- magnifying glasses;
- a minibeast tank;
- an aerator;
- a camera.

Investigating foods

Give children the chance to explore the following foods and equipment:

- fruits, including apples, pears, berries, avocado pears;
- salad, including lettuces of different varieties, cucumber, spring onions, tomatoes;
- vegetables, including potatoes, carrots, onions, turnips, cabbages, beans;
- eggs;
- wheat products, including flour and pasta;
- baking equipment, including see-through saucepans;

- a cooker to investigate the effects of heating;
- a refrigerator to investigate the effects of cooling.

Observing the weather

The following equipment will be useful:

- bubble blowers and liquid;
- soap powder for washing clothes;
- washing line and pegs for drying;
- washing-up bowl to collect rainwater, hailstones and snow;
- sticks and other objects for making shadows.

Maths

Comparing and measuring

Give children a chance to use the following:

- cups;
- jugs;
- bottles;
- handspans;
- metre rules;
- height charts;
- balance scales;
- kitchen and bathroom scales.

Investigating shape and space

Indoor equipment:

- shopping bags;
- boxes;
- suitcases.

Outdoor equipment:

- kites;
- hoops;
- balls;
- beanbags;
- wheeled toys.

Investigating number

Unbreakable plastic picnic sets with plates, mugs, knives, forks and spoons.

English

Making marks and drawing

The following equipment will be useful:

- a clipboard for outside work;
- files and folders to store drawings and mark-making;
- a notice-board;
- chalk;
- crayons;
- felt-tipped pens;
- paint;
- charcoal;
- face and fabric paints;
- a word processor.

Reading and storytelling

Children will benefit from using a wide range of resources, including:

- information, story, poetry and rhyme books;
- story cassettes with books;
- a story board with figures;
- puppets;
- big books, including those made by children and staff.